LOCAL CHURCH PLANNING MANUAL

YO-ELV-299

William Jessup University
Library
333 Sunset Blvd.
Rocklin, CA 95765

32087

LOCAL CHURCH PLANNING MANUAL

Contains All Needed Instructions and Worksheets

Richard E. Rusbuldt · Richard K. Gladden · Norman M. Green, Jr.

1/83

San Jose Bible College Library
790 S. 12th St., P.O. Box 1090
San Jose, California 95108

JUDSON PRESS® VALLEY FORGE

LOCAL CHURCH PLANNING MANUAL

Copyright © 1977
Judson Press, Valley Forge, PA 19481
Second Printing, 1978

All rights reserved. No part of this publication may be reproduced, stored in a retrieval system, or transmitted in any form or by any means, electronic, mechanical, photocopying, recording, or otherwise, without the prior permission of the copyright owner, except for brief quotations included in a review of the book.

Unless otherwise indicated, Bible quotations in this volume are in accordance with the Revised Standard Version of the Bible, copyrighted 1952 and 1971 by the Division of Christian Education of the National Council of the Churches of Christ in the United States of America, and are used by permission.

Also quoted in this book:
Good News for Modern Man, The New Testament and Psalms in Today's English Version. Copyright © American Bible Society, 1966, 1970, 1971.

Library of Congress Cataloging in Publication Data

Rusbuldt, Richard E.
    Local church planning manual.

    1. Church management—Handbooks, manuals, etc. I. Gladden, Richard K., joint author. II.   Green, Norman M., joint author. III.   Title.
BV652.R87   254   77-7109
ISBN 0-8170-0753-9

Illustrations by Paul Edwards

Users may reproduce as necessary any graphs, charts, or worksheets from the Appendix.

The name JUDSON PRESS is registered as a trademark in the U.S. Patent Office.

Printed in the U.S.A. ⊕

Preface

Local churches have long asked for help in planning. Over the years, the denominations have responded to their requests in a number of ways. As churches and denominational units planned, their experiences led to better and more complete resources and a deeper understanding of the different parts which, together, make up the whole of planning. This *Manual* is one more step along the path the church can follow in using planning to define and carry out its mission.

This *Manual* is the product of a team effort. Each of us has worked to improve ways of helping congregations plan what they should be and should do. We have come together because each wanted to make use of the skills, resources, and experiences the others could contribute.

Rusbuldt is on a regional denominational staff and is in daily contact with pastors and church members. His specialization is "leader development." Green is on the staff of a national denominational program board, working both with churches and regional units in program and administrative studies. Gladden staffs the research and planning operation of our denomination's executive office. Together we bring to this work about a half-century of experience, first as pastors and then as denominational staff.

We have not, however, produced this *Manual* alone.

We are indebted to others for the training and resources upon which we have built: Dr. Arthur M. Adams, Rev. Ralph L. Belknap, Dr. Henry E. Garrett, Rev. Lawrence H. Janssen, Rev. Richard M. Jones, Dr. William A. Koppe, Rev. Gordon R. Korb, Rev. Walter P. Parry, and Rev. Leonard A. Sibley.

We are indebted to yet others who contributed by critiquing early drafts that led to a field-test edition of this *Manual:* Dr. Myron Chartier, Dr. Richard Firster, Rev. Claude Fulks, Rev. Joseph Mason, Mr. Arthur Munson, Rev. Leland Pease, and Dr. Eugene Wright.

We are indebted to the more than seventy churches which participated in the field test, many of which shared their experiences with us.

We are indebted to *Local Church Planning Manual* Review Committee members who read and made suggestions for the manuscript as it was being prepared for publication: Rev. L. Gordon Bucy, Rev. Kenneth D. Blazier, Rev. Charles N. Forsberg, Dr. Paul O. Madsen, and Rev. C. Glenn Orr.

We are grateful to our support staff who have shared in manuscript preparation and in carrying other responsibilities, providing us the time to develop the process and write the *Manual:* Mrs. Janet Mills, Mrs. Jean Munson, Mrs. Doris Pufko, Mrs. Evelyn Stambaugh, and Mrs. Peggy Stewart.

We are grateful to our executives for encouraging us in this joint project; our thanks go to: Rev. Atha J. Baugh, Dr. Robert C. Campbell, Dr. R. Eugene Crow.

Finally, and affectionately, we thank our families for their patience, their sacrifices, and their constant support. We dedicate this *Manual* to our wives: Flossie, Jane, and Dolores.

Richard E. Rusbuldt • Richard K. Gladden • Norman M. Green, Jr.
Valley Forge, Pennsylvania • February, 1977

Contents

Introduction

Luke tells us that early in his ministry, Jesus took the Isaiah scroll and read the following words to the worshipers in Nazareth:

> "The Spirit of the Lord is upon me,
>   because he has chosen me to
>   bring good news to the poor.
> He has sent me to proclaim
>   liberty to the captives
> and recovery of sight to the blind,
> to set free the oppressed
>   and announce that the time has come
> when the Lord will save his people."
>   (Luke 4:18-19, TEV)

He concluded his reading and said, "This passage of scripture has come true today, as you heard it being read." He used these words to describe the way he would minister.

Later, Jesus called twelve disciples, trained and taught them, and sent them out. He encouraged his disciples by saying they would do even greater works than he (John 14:12).

Your church's ministry comes directly from what Jesus handed on to his disciples. The church is to bring good news to the poor. It is to proclaim liberty to captives. It is to recover sight to the blind. It is to set free the oppressed. It is to announce that the time has come when the Lord will save his people.

This *Manual* is designed to help congregations decide how they can best carry out what Christ is calling them to do. This *Manual* is a tool to help churches respond to the leading of the Holy Spirit. Your church can become an agent of freedom for many if you are willing to plan.

"Churches are sometimes like people. Some are lazy; others are hard working. Some look for Christ's direction; others ignore Christ's leadership. Some think and pray and plan; others sit and argue and fail."[1]

> If you don't know (or care)
> *where* you're going, *how* (or
> if) you get there doesn't
> matter.

There are three reasons for planning: (1) to know *where* you're going, (2) to figure out *how* to get there, (3) to know *when* you have arrived.

Many churches tend to focus on "today" and on "today's problems." Our world moves too fast for that anymore. To look at today is to run a great risk of being "out-of-focus" for tomorrow. How we see today is largely decided by decisions we made

---

[1] W. L. Howse and W. O. Thomason, *A Church Organized and Functioning* (Nashville: Convention Press, 1963), p. 8.

yesterday. Planning is a way to think about tomorrow, so when tomorrow becomes today we can be ready. Churches that plan put aside thoughts of "do what you can and hope for the best." They challenge and claim the future with confidence. Such planning can bring new vitality to the mission of a local church.

What Is Planning?

Planning is a discipline. Planning is a process. Planning has "steps" in it. Following the steps of planning is a good way to make better decisions. A good planning process will help your church discover *who* it is and *what* it is; decide *what* it should do, *how* it should do what it does, and *when*. Further, planning will help your church know how well it achieved what it wanted to accomplish.

Why Should Your Church Plan?

Perhaps you've heard others give reasons for *not* planning:[2]

Plans are out of date almost as soon as they are written down.

No one knows what tomorrow will bring—maybe opportunities, maybe disasters.

You can't predict the future; it's dangerous today to decide about tomorrow.

We can't afford the time planning takes.

The chances are people said the same thing to Noah while he was building the ark! Now, here are some reasons for planning:

1. The steps of a disciplined planning process provide more decision points in the life of your church and give the Holy Spirit more opportunities to lead you.

2. Volunteers do much of the work of a church; systematic planning helps to identify, enlist, and organize volunteers for ministry.

3. Planning helps persons to work *smarter* rather than *harder*. Planning helps us find better ways by forcing us to consider alternatives.

4. Planning encourages us to think about the future. Thinking ahead helps us be more alert to problems, opportunities, and changes that affect what we do.

5. Planning develops "keener" programs by testing the ideas of a few by the judgments of many. (Planning helps avoid the problem of only one or two persons making the decisions.)

6. The efforts people invest in a planning process build momentum to work toward common goals and related objectives. Planning helps people to know just what it is they are being asked to do.

7. Planning helps us pay attention to the results we get because of what we did. It lets us avoid simply being "busy." In short, planning provides the basis for evaluation.[3]

8. Planning can build a foundation of support. Being involved in decisions about "what to do" and "how to do" gets church members thinking and gives them a chance to "buy in" early, when their thinking can make a difference.

---

[2] Adapted from "Why Plan?" by Jeffry A. Timmons and John L. Hayes, appearing in *New Venture Creation* by Jeffry A. Timmons, Leonard E. Smollen, and Alexander L. M. Dingee, Jr. (Homewood, Ill.: Richard D. Irwin, Inc., 1977), chapter 6; used with the authors' permission.
[3] *Ibid.*, for reasons 3-7.

What Must Your Church Have in Order to Plan?

First, the leaders of your church (including your pastor) must believe that a planning process will help you work better as a congregation. They must be willing to learn how to plan. And, most of all, they must be willing to follow the discipline of the planning steps.

Planning is hard work! It is no simple shortcut to the future. In fact, the first time a church moves through a planning process, it will probably find some members saying that planning is demanding and consumes a lot of time. They will be right. "The first experience of planning in a thorough manner may well be somewhat miserable and agonizing; a frustrating experience."[4] However, those who have worked at planning have seen dead churches come alive; listless people find new energy for the Lord's work; the quality of stewardship increase; and church administration become more effective—more ministry for the money.

Every church bulletin announcing next week's events and every newsletter describing next month's activities reveal "planning" now under way in your church. This *Planning Manual* is designed to help your church think about the future in longer segments than just a week or a month. The *Manual* can help your church look at why you exist (your purpose) and work out specific day-to-day ministries to accomplish goals and/or objectives necessary for you to be faithful to your purpose.

Successful planning experiences bear witness that planning is worth the investment of time, patience, and dollars. To plan well, you will need to have motivated church leaders who are willing to look toward the future, and to include the participation of those who are concerned about the present. Appendix B will help you decide how much assistance you may need to follow this planning process.

An Overview of the Planning Process

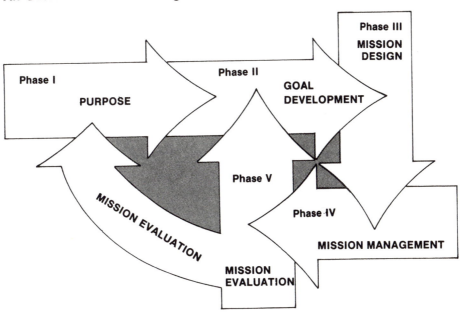

This planning process guides you step by step to say who you are, to define where you are going, to describe how you will get there, and to be aware of how far you have

---

[4] *Ibid.*

gone. It will also help you know how to be effective in the future by applying what you find out along the way.

Each of the five interlocking arrows in the diagram represents a Phase in the planning process.

Phase I Purpose—reviewing what your church is called to be and to become.

Phase II Goal Development—creating goals and objectives based on your purpose in light of all you can learn about your church, your community, and the world.

Phase III Mission Design—designing program plans and their details as the means for working toward an objective.

Phase IV Mission Management— doing the ministry of the church according to program plan details.

Phase V Mission Evaluation—drawing conclusions and making recommendations based on collected facts about what you did and what happened as a result.

Churches will require different lengths of time for the first three phases. We urge you to complete Phases I, II, and III within twelve months of the time you begin your planning. Pace your planning to take account of vacation periods (winter or summer) for your planning leaders.

Problems may arise as you use this planning process. A helpful tool, "Why Plans Fail" (and what to do about it), is included as Appendix K. However, if your whole planning process "bogs down," do not hesitate to get outside assistance (look to your denomination for help).

At the time of publication this *Manual* is the latest word in church planning. It is not the *last* word. As with everything, this resource can be improved by additional experiences. You, the reader, are requested to send us, the authors (in care of Judson Press), any comments and suggestions arising from your experience with this *Manual*.

Definitions

Area Minister—The denominational staff person responsible for churches in your geographical area (page 25).

Areas of Concern—Something about your church life, your community, or the world that calls your congregation to act because of the way your church has stated its purpose and assumptions (pages 43-44).

Assumption—What you believe to be true and are willing to act upon; makes you confident even when you lack complete information; is your judgment of what the available facts mean; is the foundation upon which your church's goals, objectives, and program plans rest (pages 39-40).

Data—Facts, statistics, or the like, either from historical records or produced by asking questions, observing, or testing (pages 32-34).

Environmental Assumptions—What you believe to be true about your community and the world (the contexts in which you live). Environmental assumptions should describe your town or city, county, and state, as well as the worldwide situations that could both affect and be affected by your congregation (page 42).

Evaluation—The act of considering carefully the worth or value of what you have done as a result of your planning (page 83).

Goal—A statement expressing a condition or "end-state" you wish to attain, a desired long-range result of ministry (page 48).

Information—An organized body of data; knowledge produced by putting data into some order and interpreting it (page 35).

Information Summary—The report in which many pieces of data are organized by agreed-upon categories. Data pieces, when related to each other and when examined carefully for meanings, can become usable information (page 35).

Objective—A clear, simple statement of a target to be reached, it is derived from a goal statement. It should be stated in such a way that movement toward achieving the goal to which it is related can be measured (page 54).

Operational Assumption—What you believe to be true about your church's traditions, organization, and ways of operating (how it goes about doing its work); what you believe about its present and future strengths and weaknesses (pages 42-43).

Phase—One of the five major clusters of planning activities (page 12).

Planning Task Force—The group of persons your church has named to direct its planning (pages 28-29).

Program Coordinator—That person who coordinates all aspects of the planned program in your church and through whom your Program Plan Managers report to the Planning Task Force (pages 80-81).

Program Plan—A blueprint describing in general how to use what you have to achieve each objective (pages 65-66).

Program Plan Details—The individual parts of a Program Plan (page 70).

Program Plan Manager—The person responsible for a Program Plan from its early stages through evaluation (pages 79-80).

Purpose—The general, comprehensive long-range reason(s) why your congregation should continue to exist (page 19).

Purpose Statement—A clear, concise description of the purpose of your church in terms of what it is to be rather than what it is to do (pages 19-20).

Step—One of the necessary planning activities within each of the five phases listed on page 12.

Theological Assumptions—What you believe to be true about what God *because of His nature* is calling His people to do *because of their nature* (pages 41-42).

Points of Entry to Planning

You, the reader (whether lay or clergy), must decide who in your church should also become familiar with this *Planning Manual.* If you are a layperson, invite your pastor to study planning with you. If you are a pastor, share this material with the lay leaders who can help you make church planning work.

You can begin *long-range planning* at two points, and *program planning* at another.

Entry A > (Long-range Planning) Begin by studying your *church's purpose.* We strongly recommend this approach since a study of your church's purpose is basic to determining what you hope to accomplish.

Some church members may not be ready to start planning by discussing purpose. They may not immediately see this as a need. Or, they may feel more secure to begin planning by looking at what they are already doing. In this case use Entry B.

Entry B⟩ Begin with Step 2:1 in the *Goal Development* Phase of the planning
(Long-range model. (This step is called "Form a Planning Task Force.") As you work
Planning) through Step 2:2 , Step 2:3 , and Step 2:4 , you will find it
important at some point to return to the purpose section (referred to in
Entry A) and complete that task before trying to write your church
goals.

The option available for church program planners is to use the work done by an
already existing Planning Task Force to move directly into Program Plans.

Entry C⟩ Program planners can enter the planning process by starting with
(Program Step 2:8 of Goal Development, "Write Goals." Those responsible for
Planning) each program (youth ministry, women's work, social concern,
evangelism, etc.) should ask the Planning Task Force for the church's
purpose statement and for any statistical and/or other information that
has been gathered and reduced to "Areas of Concern."

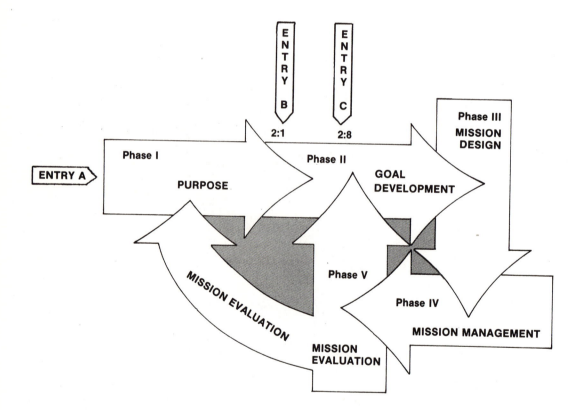

Said Alice to the Cheshire cat,
"Which way shall I go?"

Said the cat,
"Where do you want to go?"

"I don't really know," answered Alice.

I don't really know!

"Then," said the cat, "if you don't know where you want to go, it doesn't much matter which way you go, does it?"

BUT FOR US IT DOES MATTER—

. . . For Christ's Church . . .
. . . And particularly for your local church . . .

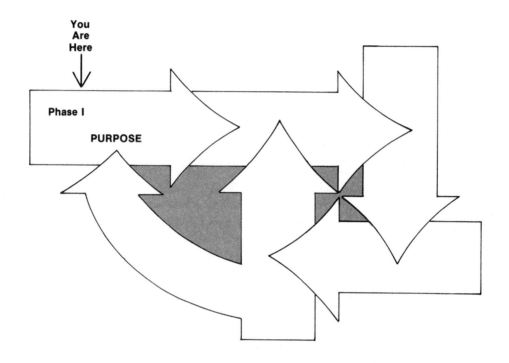

You
Are
Here

Phase I

PURPOSE

Phase I
The Purpose of Your Church

INTRODUCTION

STEP
1:0

Effective ministry is more likely to happen when church members are aware of and thoroughly familiar with the congregation's "reason for being." Everything you do (programs, ministries, stewardship, etc.) should begin with and reflect your congregation's stated purpose.

Purpose: The general, comprehensive, long-range reason(s) why your congregation should continue to exist.

Why consider the Purpose of your congregation? The first step in planning is to understand why your organization exists: what it feels it should become, or, in other words, what it must *be* to justify its existence.

A clear purpose statement *sets the stage* for all your church should do. The purpose statement becomes the basis for setting priorities, choosing programs and projects, evaluating results. A purpose statement which uses vague generalizations or which dodges issues can cripple planning. On the other hand, a clear purpose statement can focus attention and energies for action.

A clearly stated church purpose statement:

1. *Can help persons think biblically and/or theologically*

    Each church has a unique mission when compared with other institutions in society. No other institution can do your church's work!

    Good church planning carefully considers:

    the nature of the Church as revealed in the Bible;

    your local church's history and tradition; and

    its ability to grow and develop.

    It is stimulating to think theologically!

2. *Can help persons think about the world in which they minister.*

    "There's a world in need out there!"

    Some churches, however, have a hard time deciding how to do something about those needs.

    Planning begins with concern for the area or neighborhood around your church. This is where your people, buildings, and programs interact. It is where you respond with worship opportunities, education, witness, and service ministries. Depending on your church location, this may be a small geographic area embracing many people across a variety of settings (a city); or, this may be a rural situation containing few people spread over many miles of territory.

When working on your purpose statement, the Planning Task Force (or purpose writing group) should take into account what you feel *your* church is called to do. Activity simply for the sake of "being busy" has little meaning for any church. To be meaningful, your activity must be something God calls your church to do, using all your resources in the world "out there."

3. *Can help persons think about how their church operates or, perhaps, should operate.*

Many people give many hours to operate a local congregation. Your church's purpose can show the important directions of ministry that affect how your congregation operates.

Does working on a purpose statement have to take a lot of time? That depends. Some planning committees, using only a few sessions, have refined their church's purpose statement so it could be given to the congregation for review and vote. On the other hand, *reviewing-and-revising* or *writing* a purpose statement can represent three or four months of hard work. For this reason some congregations decide to carry on business as usual for several months while their planning group works to clarify its purpose statement.

Most churches have a purpose statement (or a statement of mission), usually found in their constitutions or official church documents. If not found elsewhere, every incorporated church will find a purpose statement in its Articles of Incorporation.

> If your church does not have a purpose statement, your task is clear—prepare one as your foundation for planning.
>
> Read Appendix C to get an idea of what a purpose statement can look like. Begin with Steps 1:1 , 1:2 , and 1:3 . Next, go to Step 1:6 and continue the process.
>
> When you get to Step 1:9 , follow Route 3.

How to Begin Planning by Working on Your Purpose Statement . . .

SELECT A PURPOSE STATEMENT WRITING GROUP

STEP 1:1

The first step is to name a purpose statement writing group. The group should represent the total congregation and include:

—church members who have a strong commitment to Christ and your church

—church members who are willing to invest time and energy in a process that could take several months

—a cross section of your congregation, such as college youths, single-parent families, elderly living alone, shift workers, etc.

—persons who tend to reflect on the "good old days" as well as persons who tend to look forward to change

—a chairperson with the ability to lead the group in writing a purpose statement.

Purpose writing should be a group operation, with the pastor present but not dominated by the pastor. There is no better place for your minister to give assistance in planning than as your theologian-in-residence. The pastor's job here, however, is not to do the group's thinking. Your pastor should introduce issues, provide helpful resources, and suggest procedures for working on your purpose statement.

A church purpose statement can be written either by an existing or by a newly created group. Consider the following approaches. Choose the one that seems to fit your church best.

1. Form *a special task force,* representative of the congregation, to prepare your purpose statement.

2. Use *an already existing group,* such as a church board, council, committee, or some other representative group.

3. If your church has *a one-board structure,* use that board as a total group or form a purpose statement task force from among its membership.

4. If your church has *a two-board structure,* create a task force of representatives from both boards.

5. A church with *a three (or more)-board structure* can use a modification of #4.

6. If your congregation has already decided to use systematic planning and has already named a *Planning Task Force,* use that task force.[1]

Whichever approach you choose, the group should follow the steps in Phase I. Step 1:2 is important to help your congregation understand the task your group is undertaking.

SERMON SUPPORT

STEP
1:2

During the time you work on your purpose statement, ask your pastor to deliver several sermons that deal with, "The importance of a church's purpose being up-to-date and vital so it can guide planning for the future." Ask your pastor *not* to preach on your church's current purpose statement; this will be dealt with later. You can begin Step 1:3 immediately.

YOUR CHURCH'S HISTORY

STEP
1:3

Distribute to your purpose-statement writing group a brief, up-to-date history of your church.

If you do not have one, write a brief history of your church. Ask someone who has been around awhile to outline the history; feature significant events, specific ministries, services to the community, and accomplishments. The history should touch only the highlights. More can be studied and written later. Give a copy to every member of your group.

STEP
1.4

As You Begin Actual Work on a Purpose Statement . . .
ANSWER SOME QUESTIONS ABOUT CONGREGATIONAL AWARENESS

In what areas does your church function? It probably worships, proclaims, educates, and ministers (serves others). You may see additional functions. Does most of what you do as a congregation reflect your purpose? How well do your members know your stated purpose? Ask your group to answer the following questions.

1. Do more than 50 percent of your church members know you have a statement of purpose?

Yes____ No____

2. Do more than 50 percent of your *elected leaders* know where to find your church's statement of purpose?

Yes____ No____

---

[1] See pages 28-29 for criteria to form a Planning Task Force.

3. Have your *elected leaders* studied your statement of purpose within the last two years?

Yes_____ No_____

4. Has a sermon or series of sermons been preached on your congregation's purpose during the past year?

Yes_____ No_____

5. If your congregation has specific goals, are these related to your purpose statement?

Yes_____ No_____

6. Is your purpose statement ever printed in your church bulletin?

Yes_____ No_____

7. Is your purpose statement ever featured in your newsletter?

Yes_____ No_____

8. Is your purpose statement the subject of a letter to your members at least once a year?

Yes_____ No_____

9. Does your church's budget-raising activity take account of your purpose statement?

Yes_____ No_____

10. Does your church architecture reflect your stated purposes?

Yes_____ No_____

Mostly "Yes" answers suggest your congregation is probably aware of what your church has in the past said is its reason for being (its purpose). Mostly "No" answers suggest your congregation may be unaware that you even have a stated purpose. The next task is to examine your purpose statement by moving to Step 1:5 .

STEP 1:5

STUDY YOUR STATEMENT OF PURPOSE

Ask each member of your group to examine your church's statement of purpose and answer the following questions:

1. How recently has it been revised?
2. What does each phrase or clause in the purpose statement mean to *me?*
3. Is it relevant for today?
4. Can our church move toward what the purpose statement implies?
5. Do current church programs directly reflect our purpose statement?
6. Does the statement reflect what our congregation really wants to be?
7. Does our congregation seem to have a future ministry in terms of what its purpose statement implies?
8. What does the purpose statement suggest our congregation should do which no other community or business groups are likely to do? What difference does the statement imply our congregation should make in our community?

STEP 1:6

STUDY SCRIPTURES TOGETHER

The Bible says helpful things about the purposes of the Church. It says the Church is a fellowship, a called-out community, the people of God, the body of Christ. You are a part of that Church. Read some of the following passages privately. Discuss the implications for your congregation. If you feel a Scripture passage says little to you, your church, or your group, move to another passage.

1. Exodus 3:13-17 and Matthew 28:18-20—Two "Great Commission" Scriptures
2. Isaiah 53—"The Suffering Servant"
3. Jeremiah 7:1-15—"This Is the Temple of the LORD"
4. Esther 4:14—"For Such a Time as This"
5. Mark 8:27-38—"We See and Yet Do Not Understand"
6. John 3:16-20—"The Object of God's Love"
7. John 8:31-36—"The Truth Will Make You Free"
8. John 10:7-18—"I Came That They May Have Life"
9. Romans 12:1-21—"Christian Style of Life"
10. 1 Corinthians 12:4-31—"All Members of One Body"
11. 2 Corinthians 5:16-21—"Ministry of Reconciliation"
12. Ephesians 1:1-23—"The Lordship of Christ"
13. Ephesians 4:1-16—"Christ's Gifts"
14. 1 John 2:7-11—"The Test Is Love"

Note: The Bible does not "prepackage" church purpose statements. Instead, in the Bible God gives suggestions to help us discover the purpose for each congregation's unique situation. Other Scripture passages are listed in Appendix D.

CONSIDER THIS PARABLE

STEP 1:7

> This is an optional exercise, designed to help your group discover what is meant by "basic purpose." Give each member a copy of the parable and the related questions.

A Parable

Two transportation firms, with an eye to profit, each launched a passenger ship to sail the oceans of the world. Both ships attracted customers. Each bustled with excitement and activity. For a time, both were profitable. One firm insisted on regular maintenance and from time to time added new types of service. These were costly and for several weeks each year this ship was in dry dock, cutting the number of its voyages and its firm's profits. The other company insisted their ship sail every week of the year, to return an uninterrupted profit from ticket sales. This it was able to do.

Several years passed. Slowly, a trend began to develop. Fewer people sailed on the year-round ship. The other ship, regularly dry-docked, continued to have all the passengers it could accommodate at each sailing. Conditions on the year-round ship finally reached the point where the owners were no longer able to make a profit by carrying passengers; their analysis of the changing situation soon forced them to convert the vessel from a passenger ship to one that carried only cargo.

Questions About the Parable

1. What was the purpose of both ship owners at the beginning of the parable?
2. Why did one choose to take his ship out of the water regularly for repairs, innovation, etc.?
3. List reasons that might have kept people from sailing on the year-round ship?
4. Do circumstances affect purpose?

Questions About What the Parable Implies for Planning

1. Do circumstances affect the purpose or mission of your congregation?

2. Does your church regularly evaluate and assess its mission and operation?

3. In what ways is it more difficult to get "passengers" on your "church ship" today?

> By this time you have probably recognized that the purpose of the two shipowners was to make a profit, not carry passengers. Carrying passengers was the means. The end, or purpose, was profit!

STUDY EXTREMES IN PURPOSE STATEMENTS

STEP 1:8

The way you write your purpose statement will determine the direction and style of ministry for your church. A purpose statement should help your congregation discover what should be done and provide the "push" to get it done. *How* you state your purpose is important.

Consider this sample purpose statement, "X":

> The purpose of this church, as the body of Christ in close and loving fellowship, is to maintain the holy worship of God and the spiritual nurture of our members.

This statement says that *worship for its members, a close-knit fellowship,* and *maintenance* of local church life are important. The statement will lead the church to focus on its internal life.

Consider this sample purpose statement, "Y":

> The purpose of our church is to witness to all persons that Jesus Christ, Lord and Savior, calls us to hear and to respond as His servants in the midst of human life, in the places where we work and spend our days.

This statement says the congregation should *involve itself in depth in its community* and in "other-than-local-church" concerns. The statement will *not* lead the church to maintain its support base, the local church itself.

Neither of these sample purpose statements is adequate because each represents an extreme position. Your purpose statement should provide a balance in what it emphasizes.

Further, study "Some Examples of Purpose Statements" carried in Appendix C.

WHICH ROUTE TO FOLLOW?

STEP 1:9

STOP HERE! Three routes are now open to you:

Route 1) Submit your purpose statement in its present form to your official board or congregation.

Route 2) Revise or modify your present purpose statement; then submit it to the official board or congregation.

Route 3) Write a new purpose statement which can be submitted to your official board or congregation.

Now, choose either **Route 1, Route 2,** or **Route 3.** If you select **Route 1,** move to Step 1:11 . If you select **Route 2** or **Route 3,** move to Step 1:10 .

STOP HERE !
Three routes are
now open to you..

| STEP 1:10 | **REVISE, REWRITE, OR WRITE YOUR PURPOSE STATEMENT** |

Put into simple, direct sentences why your church exists—*TODAY*. After developing a first draft statement, your group may want to set its work aside for a week or so to let it cool off before coming together to work on it again. Time away from the product of creative group work often helps understanding. It gives each group member an opportunity to think things through alone.

Guidelines for writing a purpose statement: [2]

1. Answer some basic questions:

   a. Why does your church exist?

   b. Why do you conduct worship services, church school classes, youth programs, etc.?

   c. What should your church *be* as a part of the body of Christ?

2. Make sure your purpose statement deals with the vertical relationship between your church and God.

3. Confine your thinking to *basic* reasons why your church exists, rather than including specific programs, services, or ministries. These will be dealt with later.

4. Strive for quality and honesty; do not be overly concerned if you feel you do not have a perfect purpose statement. As you gain more experience in planning, you will become more expert in stating your church's purpose. (The purpose statement can be reviewed at the end of the evaluation, Phase V Step 5:5 .)

NOTE! If your group has difficulty in developing its purpose statement, get some help. Do not hesitate to ask your area minister,[3] other denominational staff, or resource persons in your community to assist you. This is a critical step! Don't give up!

| STEP 1:11 | **SEEK REACTIONS** |

When you have completed your draft of the purpose statement, we suggest you review it in light of Step 1:8 . Then, refer it to your area minister for reaction and counsel. Consider what your area minister says as you prepare your final draft.

Invite your area minister to react to the written purpose before submitting it to the parent body.

---

[2] If needed, you will find several examples of purpose statements in Appendix C. Including them does not in any way suggest that these could or should be used by your church; they are offered only as suggestions to stimulate your thinking.

[3] The denominational staff person responsible for churches in your geographical area.

STEP
1:12

ADOPT AND REFER YOUR STATEMENT

Keep working on the statement until your group is satisfied with the way it is worded. Take time to revise or rewrite until agreement is reached.

When your group has agreed on the statement it wants to refer, forward that statement to the appropriate board or council for consideration. Supply any background information needed to explain the process you used to develop the statement.

STEP
1:13

PRESENTING THE PROPOSED PURPOSE STATEMENT

The purpose statement, once approved by the appropriate board or council, should be submitted to your congregation for discussion, modification (if necessary), and action to accept or reject.[4] Some denominations do not require congregational approval of policy. However, all churches will find it helpful in planning to take this step.

STEP
1:14

AFTER APPROVAL

Three things should happen NEXT.

1. *Communicate the purpose statement.* Use all available methods and media to communicate the purpose statement to your members on a continuing basis. For example, your purpose statement can be the subject for an adult elective course in your church school; it can be used for small group study; every class held for new members should contain some study of purpose; a slide set on your church's purpose can be prepared for use by classes, organizations, committees, boards, etc.

2. *Use the purpose statement in preaching.* After the purpose statement is adopted, your pastor should be invited to deliver several sermons on it, laying groundwork for continuing the planning process. One way would be to use a full month when the new purpose statement is the subject of the Sunday morning sermons. The first sermon could be the responsibility of the pastor; the second could be assigned to a laywoman or layman; the third could be assigned to another layperson (of the opposite sex from the previous person), and the fourth sermon again by the pastor.

3. *Use the purpose statement in planning.* As you move through this planning process, use the purpose statement where it is called for.

---

[4] If the congregation should happen not to accept the purpose statement, your group can do one of two things: (1) it can "go back to the drawing board" and try again, or (2) it can ask to be dismissed with appreciation so another group can be named to carry on the work.

Phase II
Goal Development

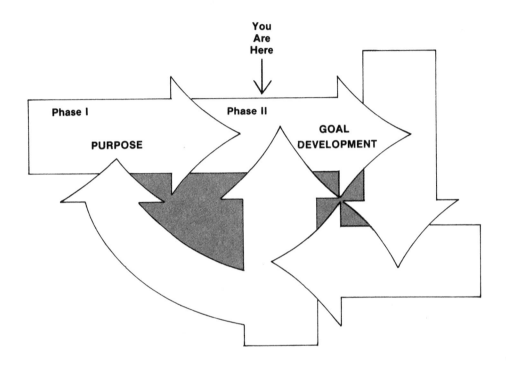

INTRODUCTION

STEP 2:0

Once you have an approved Purpose Statement, you are ready to move to Goal Development, the second phase of the planning process. There are ten steps in Goal Development:

Step 2:1 Form a Planning Task Force

Step 2:2 Look at Your Present Situation

Step 2:3 Gather Data About Your Church, Community, and World

Step 2:4 Prepare an Information Summary

Step 2:5 Compare Your Feelings and Facts

Step 2:6 List Your Assumptions

Step 2:7 Identify Needs and Concerns

Step 2:8 Write Goals

Step 2:9 Write Objectives

Step 2:10 Set Priorities Among Objectives

The chairperson, your pastor, and other Planning Task Force members should become familiar with all ten steps prior to your first meeting. It may be possible for you to make some advance assignments, particularly Step 2:3 , to speed up the gathering of data. If you do this, be sure to brief all task force members on the content of Step 2:3 and the reason for the advance assignments.

Involving many persons in the planning process multiplies opportunities for "ownership" on the part of all church members. Encourage your members to provide input; involve as many persons as possible in Step 2:3 , the data-gathering step.

The planning decisions you make as you follow this manual *depend especially on the thoroughness with which you complete the first seven steps of Goal Development.*

STEP
2:1

FORM A PLANNING TASK FORCE

The first step is to form a "Planning Task Force."[1] The following checklist will guide you in selecting task force members.

Who, in our church, is best qualified to serve on a planning task force?

CHECKLIST FOR SETTING UP A PLANNING TASK FORCE

1. Select persons who can accept an assignment and stay with it until it is completed. (If someone must drop out in the middle of the process, it will be

[1] If you already formed a "Planning Task Force" to carry out Phase I, proceed to Step 2:2 .

extremely difficult for the replacement person to "get into" what is taking place.)

2. Select persons who are willing to attend a number of extra meetings during the next three to six months.

3. Select persons who, together, represent *all* your church's membership: the youth, the elderly, those with different life-styles, etc. (If possible, more than one young person should be included in order to provide peer support.)

4. Select persons with positive feelings toward your church as well as persons who may be somewhat negative. *All* points of view should be represented.

5. Select persons who are willing to work through problems to reach some solution. (Compromise may be necessary for many task force decisions.)

6. Select persons who exhibit a strong commitment to Christ and His Church.

*How can our pastor help to
strengthen the planning process?*

7. Select enough persons, but not too many. A task force should not have less than four or more than twelve persons, including the pastor. The following scale gives some suggested sizes:

If your church has:	*Select as your task force:*
up to 50 members	3 persons plus pastor
51 to 150 members	4 persons plus pastor
151 to 300 members	7 persons plus pastor
301 to 500 members	9 persons plus pastor
beyond 500 members	11 persons plus pastor

8. The individual you choose to serve as chairperson should have the administrative ability needed to help the task force to function effectively. The chairperson should be designated by the same group which appoints the task force.[2]

9. In multiple staff churches, perhaps more than one of the professional staff should be asked to serve.

Once your task force has been appointed, you are ready to begin Step 2:2 .

Note:
It is important that task force members come to know one another on a first-name basis. Persons on the Planning Task Force will be working together for a number of months. Provide time for them to get acquainted. Schedule at least one-half hour to do this in your first meeting. Also, ask the chairperson and/or your pastor to present a devotional based on one of the Scripture passages listed on page 23.

---

[2] It may be helpful to select co-chairpersons in larger situations; they can provide support for each other.

Using newsprint on the wall or a chartstand gets your ideas up so all can focus on them.

LOOK AT YOUR PRESENT SITUATION

Two questions are basic here:
- What is your church currently doing?
                  and
- How do you feel about what your church is doing?

1. *WHAT IS YOUR CHURCH CURRENTLY DOING?*

Have on hand a supply of newsprint or other large-sized paper. Put this on an easel or a wall, using masking tape. Ask someone from your group to serve as scribe at the newsprint. Provide a broad-tip felt marker so what is written is clearly visible to all.

Write on newsprint a list of what your church is presently doing.[3] (Leave at least two inches between the items on the list. You will use this space later.) List services, ministries, programs—everything your Planning Task Force members can think of as "one of the things we do." Remember that all officers, staff, boards, committees, and organizations are involved in doing the work of the church.

In addition, individual church members perform services and ministries at the church and in their homes and community. For instance: "Three teens sing in an ecumenical singing group." "Mary Smith conducts a Wednesday morning Bible study group in her home." "John Jones tutors children after school." Etc. Be sure to include these.

You are probably doing more things than you realize; so the list will be long. At this stage, don't waste time debating unless something suggested *obviously* doesn't belong on the list.

What am I doing in this community?

---

[3] If your task force is larger than seven or eight persons, form two subgroups to work at this task. Then compare the results.

2. *HOW DO YOU FEEL ABOUT WHAT YOUR CHURCH IS DOING?*

Human feelings are significant in every aspect of church and community life. Feelings both create and reveal the "climate" of a church. Each church has its own climate. Walk into a worship service and you can feel it. In some churches there is warmth, openness, excitement, while others seem rigid, cold, and dull.

Have you heard comments like these about your church or some other?

—I felt as if I were truly in the presence of God in church this morning.

—The singing is so slow I feel like falling asleep.

—I'm bored with church school.

—They made me feel as if they were glad I came.

In each case what is said is based on how the person feels about someone or something in the church.

Feelings are important. The feelings of your Planning Task Force members as well as those of your church family should be considered as you plan the future of your church. You are encouraged to use the Satisfaction Rating Scale described below. The results will give you some indication of what data should be gathered in Step 2:3 .

Satisfaction Rating Scale

Turn to what has been written on the newsprint. Put a letter before each item. Each member of your task force, working individually, should write on a piece of paper the letter identifying each item and a number from 1 to 10 to rate how he or she feels about *each* item. For instance, a "10" expresses satisfaction with the way the program or ministry is being done, while a "5" indicates a "so-so" feeling about it. A "1" indicates dissatisfaction with an item.

Illustration of the rating scale:

1 2	3 4 5 6 7 8	9 10
Dissatisfaction	Average "so-so"	Satisfaction

As an example, you may rate an item with a 7, indicating that you feel more than "so-so" about it. To another you may give a 3, implying that better performance is needed before you will begin to feel satisfied.

Express your feelings honestly. Some of the things your church is doing may not rate very high. This is normal. You will have an opportunity in later steps to consider what to do about items with low ratings.

Example:

NEWSPRINT LISTING	*INDIVIDUAL WORK SHEET*
a. Morning worship service	*a.* 9
b. Maintaining our building	*b.* 4
c. Senior high youth group	*c.* 2
d. Meals on Wheels	*d.* 8
e. Senior choir	*e.* 7
f. Evangelistic program	*f.* 3
Etc.	Etc.

Ask each person to go to the newsprint and under each item place the number he or she gave to it. *To arrive at a group score for each item,* total all the numbers and divide by the number of persons who participated. Write the result on the right side of the newsprint and draw a circle around it. Do this for each item.

Example:

```
┌─────────────────────────────────────────────────┐
│  THINGS WE ARE DOING . . .        Av. Grade       │
│  a. Morning worship service                       │
│     8, 7, 9, 8, 7, 3, 6, 9, 7          ( 7 )       │
│  b. Maintaining our building                      │
│     9, 10, 10, 8, 7, 10, 8, 9, 9       (8.9)       │
│  c. Senior high youth group                       │
│     2, 3, 2, 1, 4, 4, 3, 3, 4          (2.9)       │
│  d. Meals on Wheels                               │
│     7, 9, 9, 10, 9, 8, 9, 9, 8         (8.7)       │
│  e. Senior choir                                  │
│     1, 3, 4, 5, 2, 3, 3, 4, 5          (3.3)       │
│  f. Evangelistic program                          │
│     8, 7, 6, 9, 10, 8, 7, 6, 6         (7.4)       │
│     Etc.                                          │
└─────────────────────────────────────────────────┘
```

When you have finished this rating, the numbers placed after each item will give a general picture of how you feel about what your church is doing, the particular things you feel good about, and the things about which you feel less than satisfied.

Remember, this type of exercise indicates *only* how your Planning Task Force feels about the various things your church is doing. Interviewing some church members will help you check how well you represent the overall feelings of your congregation.

STEP 2:3

GATHER DATA ABOUT YOUR CHURCH, COMMUNITY, AND WORLD

To plan carefully, you need facts. Your church's ability to make responsible decisions about its future depends on how well the Planning Task Force secures accurate data about your church, its community, and the world.

Step 2:3 will take time and hard work. First efforts to collect facts always take more time than later efforts. In later planning it will be necessary only to update your existing data. Therefore, your Planning Task Force should invest now the time and energy required to collect the data recommended in this *Manual.*

Three kinds of data should be gathered to provide a base for making decisions:

1. Local church data
2. Community data
3. World data

Read through all the material for this step. At the end, on page 35 you will find instructions on how to gather the data described.

The forms and instruments included in this *Manual*[4] for your use in collecting data are listed below:

1. LOCAL CHURCH DATA

To discover present and future church needs, you should be aware of membership characteristics.

[4] Appendix pages are shown in the lists. These Appendix pages are tear sheets which can be removed for your use.

a. Church and Church School Membership Table—Twenty Years (page 155)
—Membership line graph (page 157)
—Church School line graph (page 159)

b. Membership Gain or Loss Table—Twenty Years (page 161)
—Membership Methods bar graph (page 163)

c. Church School Profile of current enrollment and average attendance (page 165)
—Church School Profile graph (page 167)

d. Money Received—Twenty Years (page 169)
—Financial Support line graph (page 171)

e. Contribution Table by Family Units (page 173)
—Weekly Giving Profile graph (page 175)

f. Distribution of the Church Dollar (page 177)
—Circle graph (page 177)

g. Church Participation Profile (page 179)
—Church participation cards (sample card, page 180) may be secured in quantity from National Ministries, American Baptist Churches, U.S.A., Valley Forge, PA 19481.
—Tabulate results on summary and age-sex distribution pages (pages 183, 185, 187, 189)
—Age–Sex Distribution bar graph (page 191)

h. Church History (page 213)

i. Church Program Review (Appendix E)
—Assign the task of writing reviews of church programs to each appropriate *unit* (or group) in your church. Follow the questions provided.

*j. Exploring Membership Attitudes: A Questionnaire Service (Appendix M)[5]
—Questionnaire for Local Church Planning (See Appendix M)

*k. Role Expectations Checklist (Appendix L)
—A selected list of items related to the total ministry of the church—to be responded to by the pastor and the laity to help determine the expectation levels of each other.

* l. Interviews
—Interviews can be conducted with both active and inactive members. It is as important to learn how inactive members feel about your church as it is to listen to those who are present every Sunday.

2. *COMMUNITY DATA*

Define your community in terms of its natural and man-made limits. Sometimes natural communities are easily recognized by local residents; at other times they are not. Within large cities, communities usually do not extend for more than a few square blocks, while in smaller cities they may encompass the entire city and some of the surrounding rural territory. In rural areas a community will quite frequently cover a township. In some sparsely settled areas the entire county will virtually be a community surrounding the county seat. Highways, means of travel, attitudes toward distance, and group identification are important in determining the area which can be called your church's community.

To define your community, consider the "effective service area" of your church. A basic question to ask is, "From what part of the area around our building can we reasonably expect to draw people to participate in our program?" Another basic question is, "How far does our influence extend?"

Gather data about the community you have defined as your effective service

[5] Items with asterisks are optional.

area. One of your best sources is the U.S. census. The Census Bureau publishes a wealth of information. How to get and use these materials is described in Appendix G. The following forms for collecting community data are found in Appendix F on pages 193-205.

a. Church Area and Neighborhood: Population Characteristics (page 193)
—Neighborhood Population Table (page 195)

b. Employment Groups (page 197)

c. Age-Sex Distribution, Area and Neighborhood Population (page 199)
—Age–Sex Distribution: Area bar graph (page 201)
—Age–Sex Distribution: Neighborhood bar graph (page 203)

d. Housing in Church Neighborhood and Area (page 205)

e. Community Interviews (Appendix H)
—50 possible interviews which can provide information to your Planning Task Force: sample questions or topics are included with each.

f. Where Members and Constituents Live
(top half of page 209)
—Distance from Building bar graph (page 211)

g. Maps (pages 207-208)
—Family or Household Membership Map
*—Evangelism Map[6]
*—Church Location and Community Factors Map

*h. Where New Members Lived When They Joined
(bottom half of page 209)

3. *WORLD DATA*

International jet travel has convinced most of us that "it's a small, small world." Each church should be aware of how global issues and concerns affect it and how its ministry can influence them. We all have learned how a country on the other side of the world can raise oil prices and produce a chain of events that affect our families, our church's giving pattern, our church attendance, etc. Such direct links between "them" and "us" make us conscious that in the church we should be aware of global concerns and needs and what response we should make in light of the gospel.

Together, the churches of your denomination already have a worldwide perspective expressed through international missions. Such work must be continued. Now your church needs to expand its vision, examine all the needs on the world scene, and determine your response. The forms to be completed for this world data section are found in Appendix I.

At this point, make the following decisions:

First, establish a completion date for Step 2:3 .

Second, schedule some dates between now and then when your Planning Task Force can meet to report progress on its data gathering and to review this work. Ask members to protect these meeting dates in their personal calendars.

Third, after studying the options for Step 2:3 , determine how much time and energy you can invest in collecting the data necessary to make good decisions.

Your Planning Task Force must make the final decision about which and how much data should be gathered. The more thorough your data gathering, the more successful your planning will be.

Fourth, decide which of the forms and instruments described on pages 32-34 you will use. Check to see if any task force members have special interests or preferences

---

[6] Items with asterisks are optional.

in working with certain forms. Divide the work so all members are involved, either individually or in small groups. Make sure each type of data you have decided to gather is assigned to an individual or group. Enlist other resource persons in your church to help you (e.g., ask your church clerk to get twenty-year attendance and membership figures; ask the church school secretary for church school statistics, etc.). World data might be handled best by your Planning Task Force working as a total group.

PREPARE AN INFORMATION SUMMARY

STEP 2:4

In the previous two steps of Goal Development, your Planning Task Force identified and evaluated current church programs and ministries, and collected data about your church, its community, and the world. You should now create an "Information Summary" from the facts and opinions you have gathered.

Prepare your Information Summary by acting on your answers to the following two questions:

- Who on your Planning Task Force should organize the data?
  1. You could do this work as a committee of the whole.
  2. Two or three of your members with a particular interest in this step could volunteer.
  3. Your chairperson could appoint a subcommittee. (A minimum of three persons should serve, regardless of the size of your task force.)

  The amount of data gathered may require several work sessions to get it ready for the Planning Task Force meeting at which it will be used.
- What is the best way to organize the data? (Use one of the following options or create one of your own.)

  Option 1—*Place under each of the following categories the information related to it.*[7]

    a. Developing spiritually vital church members.

    b. Expanding educational ministries.

    c. Performing Christ's work in the community.

    d. Sharing Christ with unbelievers.

    e. Extending our mission throughout the world.

    f. Making our church life more productive and efficient through improved operations.

  All statistics, interview answers, program evaluations, and other material that belong to one of the six categories should be pulled together into one block of information. Some data may relate to more than one category; put these data under *each* category to which they relate.

  Option 2—*Sort the material according to its own general type, something like this:*

    a. Statistical data: counts taken on church membership, youth activities, records of church finances, the community age-sex profile, housing starts, changes in community population, etc.

    b. Program reviews and evaluations: information from boards and committees related to your church's program.

    c. Interviews: Opinions expressed by program leaders, community leaders, etc.

    d. Self-study findings: Task Force findings from Step 2:2 covering:

---

[7] Note: Examples and illustrations that follow page 46 in this *Manual* use the categories of Option 1.

What you are doing, and how you feel about what you are doing; other findings: church participation survey, questionnaire for local church planning, role-expectation checklist, etc.

Before you begin either of these two options, set a date for the Planning Task Force meeting at which you will begin work on Step 2:5 or Step 2:6 . This date will become the target for your information organizers to complete their work.

Now, begin work on your Information Summary.

STEP 2:5

COMPARE YOUR FEELINGS AND FACTS (An Optional Step)

Now, go back to the material on newsprint from Step 2:2 .

Most of what you have listed on newsprint can be checked out by looking at what your data gathering has shown *is* happening *versus* what you *believed* to be happening. Expand what you have done by using a combination of facts from your Information Summary as well as the feelings you identified in Step 2:2 to test the *value* and *participation* for each item on the newsprint. Consider that feelings, though important, cannot be the only (or final) criteria for planning. For instance, there may be 150 persons attending your morning worship service. You may feel this is very good. However, if the potential attendance is 500 because of your neighborhood and community, your feelings may cause you to miss the opportunity before you.

To test the value and participation for each item, you will need to create a work sheet similar to the examples shown on pages 37-38. Use your list from Step 2:2 adding any new items you have listed in your Information Summary.

VALUE: Based on the information you have gathered, you can now give a value to every service, ministry, and program your church offers. These have a value to your church. They have a value to the community. How much value do you attach to each thing you are presently doing? Is the value of each service, ministry, and program listed on the newsprint equal to your Planning Task Force's expectations? To your congregation's? To those of the community?

Set a value for each item on a scale of 1 to 100. Then, for the same item, multiply by 10 the Satisfaction Rating Scale score found in Step 2:2 . Compare the result with your new value. Did the score change because of what you discovered through your Information Summary? Does this comparison of the two scores suggest you should modify your value score?

When your Planning Task Force has agreed on the values for each item, write them on your worksheet.

PARTICIPATION: "Value" was given scores based on your *feelings.* "Participation," on the other hand, is based on: (1) your estimate of the potential number of persons who could be involved in the program being considered; and (2) your record of the actual number who participated, as given in your Information Summary.

How much of your constituency is involved in the various aspects of your church's mission? Does a small core group of leaders do most of the leading (work)? Sometimes it is discovered that no more than one-fourth to one-third of a church's total membership is actually busy; the rest are basically uninvolved in mission. Such an untapped pool of people could easily provide the resources, talents, and energy to meet goals you never before dreamed were possible.

Some items, however, do not need a participation section, as illustrated by Example B. Now, wherever they apply, fill in the participation scores on your worksheet.

Here are some examples:

Example A. MORNING WORSHIP
      VALUE to congregation _____ Grade (1-100)   70

           Specify: "Meaningful"; _____

                    "Meets my needs"; _____

                    "Feel good when I leave"; _____

                    "Too long"; etc. _____

      VALUE to community _____ Grade (1-100)   40

      PARTICIPATION: Potential (membership) 130

                    Participants (weekly)   43   Percentage   33

      TOTALS: 70 + 40 + 33 = 143   Average = $\dfrac{143}{3}$ = 47.67   or 48

Example B. MAINTAINING OUR BUILDING
      VALUE to congregation _____ Grade (1-100)   95

           Specify: "Lovely sanctuary"; _____

                    "new pulpit furniture" _____

      VALUE to community _____ Grade (1-100)   10

      TOTALS: 95 + 10 = 105   Average = $\dfrac{105}{2}$ = 52.5   or 53

Example C. SENIOR HIGH YOUTH GROUP
      VALUE to congregation _____ Grade (1-100)   40

           Specify: _____

      VALUE to youth _____ Grade (1-100)   25

           Specify: "Poor attendance—bored— _____

                    nothing to do" _____

      VALUE to community _____ Grade (1-100)   10

      PARTICIPATION: Potential (membership) 25

                    Participants (weekly)   4   Percentage   16

      TOTALS: 40 + 25 + 10 + 16 = 91   Average = $\dfrac{91}{4}$ = 22.7   or 23

Example D.   MEALS ON WHEELS

    VALUE to congregation _____ Grade (1–100)   60

        Specify: "Helps our shut-ins who live alone"

    VALUE to community _____ Grade (1–100)   90

    PARTICIPATION: Potential (membership)   12

                Participants (weekly)   10   Percentage   83

    TOTALS: 60 + 90 + 83 = 233   Average = $\dfrac{233}{3}$ = $\underline{\underline{77.7}}$ or 78

Example E. SENIOR CHOIR

    VALUE to congregation _____ Grade (1–100)   90

        Specify: "excellent voices"; "young

        and old"; "variety of anthems"

    VALUE to community (community hymn sings) ____ Grade (1–100)   90

    PARTICIPATION: Potential (membership)   30

                Participants (weekly)   10   Percentage   33

    TOTALS: 90 + 90 + 33 = 213   Average = $\dfrac{213}{3}$ = $\underline{\underline{71}}$

Example F.   EVANGELISTIC PROGRAM

    VALUE to congregation _____ Grade (1–100)   15

        Specify: "Too passive"; "Few actively

        involved"

    VALUE to community _____ Grade (1–100)   5

    PARTICIPATION: Potential (membership)   130

                Participants   6   Percentage   5

    TOTALS: 15 + 5 + 5 = 25   Average = $\dfrac{25}{3}$ = $\underline{\underline{8.3}}$ or 8

As shown in the examples, add the scores you have given for each value to the percent score you gave for participation. Divide by the number of scores in the item. The result will be your value and participation rating for the item. Make a new list of your items so that the one with the highest score is at the top, the one with the next highest score is second; continue doing this through all items so your list shows the item with the lowest score at the bottom.

When you have completed this step, you will have a picture of how effective your church's services, ministries, and programs are at the present time. Your new listing can be a resource for the work you will do in Step 2:6 .

<table>
<tr><td>STEP
2:6</td></tr>
</table>

LIST YOUR ASSUMPTIONS: *What Do You Believe About Your God, Your Church, Your World?*

Refer to the work you have done in earlier steps to help you spell out what you believe:
- about the task to which God is calling you as a congregation (See your Statement of Purpose.)
- about the environment in which you will minister to answer the call (See your Information Summary.)
- about how your church does/will operate to do its mission (See your final list from Step 2:5).

WHAT IS AN ASSUMPTION?

An *assumption* . . .
—is what you believe to be true and are willing to act upon.
—makes you confident even when you lack complete information.
—is your judgment of what the available facts mean.
—is the foundation upon which your church's goals, objectives, and program plans rest.

It is important to examine what you assume or believe to be true before you begin to write any goals for your church. A belief can be expressed as one of three kinds of assumptions: theological assumptions, environmental assumptions, and operational assumptions.

It is important that all members of your task force understand the term "assumption."

AN EVERYDAY-LIFE ILLUSTRATION

Everyday life is based on assumptions. We don't always check each one because that would take too much time; however, when we assume something wrong, trouble can start! Here is a personal illustration:

One winter my 2½-year-old son accompanied me on some afternoon pastoral calls. I don't like to struggle with little boy's boots, so I had been carrying him through the snow between each house and the car. When we came home from the visits, I carried him to the porch of the parsonage and placed him on his feet at the door. The winter wind was near gale force. When I finally got the door open, I expected him to go in, but all he did was lean forward. I suggested, in competition with the howling wind, that we ought to go in, to which the only response was an inquiring look and a little more leaning.

Shouting over the wind, I suggested to him that if he didn't move, I was going to help him by placing a hand "he knew where." Still fighting the wind and the door (while heating the out-of-doors), I raised my hand to offer some persuasion at the proper place, and in so doing saw something. One of his shoestrings was untied, and I was standing on it! He couldn't have moved even if he had wanted to!

When I checked my assumptions, I discovered a fact that changed the whole situation. (Can you spot my wrong assumption?)[8]

---
[8] I had assumed he had full control over both feet.

39

Clarifying basic assumptions early can avoid many conflicts down the road.

1. *CLARIFY YOUR ASSUMPTIONS*

Each church member has a set of assumptions. At times church members may have different assumptions about the same thing. It is important to provide opportunities to discuss these differences to bring about better understanding. As you can imagine, even mild disagreements on basic assumptions, if not recognized and taken into account, can mean trouble for your church.

Assumptions can express our beliefs both about how things are presently and about how things will be in the future. For instance, considering what you know now, what do you think your neighborhood will be like five years from now? Do you expect things to remain as they are? Or, do you anticipate changes that will require corresponding change in the mission of your church? What world developments do you expect to call for a change in your church's thrust and style of mission?

Today a church must be active, flexible, and competitive to have a vital influence within the world it is called to serve. In the midst of rapid social and environmental changes, no church can deal well with today's problems by using yesterday's assumptions—as if change was not taking place. To do so condemns any church's future to be simply a faster repetition of its past.

We, of course, cannot be *certain* about the future. However, to avoid repeating automatically in the future what your church has been doing, you should from time to time update or reaffirm your assumptions: the *theological,* the *environmental,* and the *operational.*

2. *STUDY SOME EXAMPLES*

Example: Loyal (and well-meaning) members of some local church boards of Christian education deal over and over again with plans for Rally Day, a Christmas party, a summer picnic, and Easter egg hunts. Such boards rarely discuss crucial issues, such as the quality of church school teaching, the nature of student interest, or the kind of support system needed by those who teach. Boards that look only at Rally Days, special parties, etc., probably work from some of the following assumptions.

—We will always have a church school.

—Our congregation expects special seasonal programs.

—Anyone we recruit to teach is automatically capable of doing the job.

—Even though our community is changing, the difference will not require changes in what we offer through our church school.

—Most of our "kids" will not drop out of church school.

—God expects special programs in church school.

—All church schools have declining attendance; so our decline is normal.

Example: Diaconate boards often think of themselves as evangelistic, the spiritual leaders in their church. Yet many boards appear to operate on such assumptions as:

—If we keep our church open, God will give an increase.

—It's the pastor's job to win people; we pay him to do this kind of work.

—Our attendance will stay about where it is, no matter what we do.

—We should put our own house in order before going outside our congregation to reach others.

—If we only had some training, we could share our faith, but we haven't, so . . .

—People today really aren't interested in either the gospel or the local church.

Note, that in these examples all three types of assumptions were included: *theological, environmental,* and *operational.*

3. *WRITE YOUR THEOLOGICAL ASSUMPTIONS*[9]

Theological Assumptions are statements about what you believe God *because of His nature* is calling His people to do *because of their nature.* Valid theological assumptions are your deepest feelings able to be acted upon. In other words, theological assumptions relate to how you intend to act. Some discussion-starter questions are: What do *you* believe about God? On what do *you* base *your* religious beliefs? What do *you* believe about Jesus Christ? What do *you* believe about the Bible that causes you to take certain actions? What is the role of prayer in *your* life? Here are some examples of theological assumptions:

a. God exists.

b. God creates.

c. God cares for His creation.

d. Jesus Christ, God's Son, died for our sins to establish fellowship between us and God.

e. The Church expresses God's love and forgiveness and is the symbol and sign that God has brought hope and healing to persons through Jesus Christ.

f. The Bible is the authority for what we believe.

g. The Holy Spirit witnesses to our spirits within and beyond the Scriptures.

h. God wants us to be involved in the world's healing.

i. Attending church regularly strengthens persons spiritually. (Worship puts power in persons' lives.)

-----

[9] An option is to divide your task force into three groups and to work on the three categories of assumptions at the same time.

j. God has a job for our church to do where we are right now.

k. The love of God, revealed in Jesus Christ, is for all persons who confess their sins and ask forgiveness.

l. The Holy Spirit gives power to any who seek to do God's will.

List your theological assumption statements on newsprint. Save for future reference.

4. *WRITE YOUR ENVIRONMENTAL ASSUMPTIONS*

Environmental Assumptions are what *you believe to be true* about your community and the world, the contexts in which you live. Environmental assumptions should describe your town or city, county, and state, as well as the worldwide situations that could both affect and be affected by your congregation. Here are some environmental assumptions:

a. The average wage level in our area will go up (two new industries are moving in, and our closed coal mines will be reopened soon).

b. There will be a shorter work week within the next five years.

c. Within the next decade, the neighborhood immediately surrounding our church will *not* be an ideal place for families with young children.

d. _____ percent of the residents in our immediate community will be retired by 19____.

e. A year-round schedule will soon be used in our public schools.

f. More families will require some kind of day-care assistance for young children by 19____.

g. Within five years, changing family patterns will force us to create new educational patterns and settings or go out of the business of Christian education.

h. By 19____, there will be _____ percent more retirees and older adults in our community with empty time on their hands.

List your environmental assumptions on newsprint. Save for future reference.

5. *WRITE YOUR OPERATIONAL ASSUMPTIONS*

Operational Assumptions are what you believe to be true about your church's *traditions, organization,* and *ways of operating* (how it goes about doing its work). What do you believe is true now and/or will be true in the future about your facilities, professional staff, lay leadership, budget, the methods you use to administer your church and carry out its ministries? Some examples are:

a. Our church will grow spiritually and numerically.

b. Our church will possess an increased sense of responsibility for ministry in its neighborhood.

c. Our next pastor will receive a housing allowance to buy his or her own home.

d. Our budget will double in the next six years.

e. Our congregation will fall apart because of an increasing unwillingness of lay persons to accept designated leadership positions.

f. Our church will be in a new building program by 19____.

g. Five years from now, by maintaining our present rate of growth, we will need additional professional staff.

h. Five years from now we will have enough money to support both a full-time pastor and a full-time associate pastor.

i. By 19____, _____ percent of our membership under fifty years of age will live more than three miles from our church building.

j. A day-care center will be started by our church.

k. We will have more types of family programs by 19_____.

l. In the next decade, our major membership growth will come through receiving members from neighborhood minority groups.

List your operational assumptions on newsprint. Save for future reference.

6. *FURTHER INSTRUCTIONS*

Make arrangements to share your assumptions with each of the church's boards and committees. Make copies of the lists. Ask each Planning Task Force member to do two things: (1) give a copy to every member of the board(s) or committee(s) for which he or she acts as the contact; (2) meet with the board or committee to review and expand the assumption lists and to find out its level of agreement with each assumption. Point out that assumptions become the base from which to write goals. Take all responses back to your Planning Task Force for summarizing and study.

Publish the summarized assumptions in your church newsletter or other media. Explain them to your total membership. Ask them to make suggestions about the list. Ask church classes, small groups, and other organizations to discuss the assumptions. Try to build participation into this step of the planning process.

IDENTIFY NEEDS AND CONCERNS

STEP
2:7

When you have completed Step 2:6, both your Information Summary and your listing of assumptions will be available to the Planning Task Force as it begins one of the most significant steps in planning—writing your church's goals. The chairperson and the pastor should prepare for Step 2:7 by selecting appropriate Scriptures which can help define areas of concern. For instance, what were some concerns of Jesus and what caused these concerns as illustrated in the verse "Jesus wept" (John 11:35)?

Begin Step 2:7 by asking, "What do our assumption lists say about us as a church?" How you go about fulfilling your purpose will depend on how you see the needs of your members, your community, and the world. Review your assumptions to identify your congregation's major areas of concern.

An *Area of Concern* is something about your church life, your community, or the world that calls your congregation to act because of the way your church has stated its purpose and assumptions. Now that you have summarized your data (your Information Summary) and prepared your assumptions in light of them, begin to look within the data for indications of:

- Issues
- Problems
- Opportunities/Challenges
- Needs

Each of these four items can be a signpost directing you to an area of concern: *Issues*—An issue is a situation in the life of your church or community about which persons have taken positions, for or against. Issues may involve personal relationships, social circumstances, finances, or other tensions. It takes courage to raise sensitive issues.

Problems—A problem is a condition demanding solution. Problems, whether in the church, the community, or both, cannot be ignored when doing long-range planning. Planning in your church depends on your refusal to ignore problems and your willingness to work at solving them!

Opportunities/Challenges—Some circumstances remain largely untreated until the *church* takes the initiative to respond. The very nature of such circumstances invites church involvement (for example, sponsoring refugees). We call these circumstances "opportunities," or sometimes, "challenges."

Needs—Needs are situations requiring relief. Needs can touch individuals, families, groups, organizations, and the environment. Needs are both local and worldwide. Institutions often find renewed vitality by searching for and responding to real needs.

A *problem* may represent someone's *need* which, at the same time, can be an *opportunity* or *challenge* for your church's ministry. Items from your Information Summary or assumption lists define an Area of Concern.

In a diagram, it might look like this:

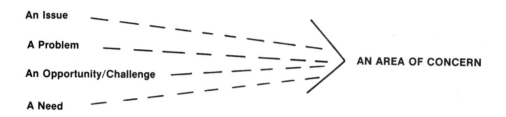

An Issue

A Problem

An Opportunity/Challenge   AN AREA OF CONCERN

A Need

A Worship Example

Suppose your purpose statement says, "God invites us to experience a personal relationship with Him expressed through worship." Suppose your Task Force has discovered from its data gathering that a substantial number of persons (members and neighbors) do not worship regularly because they "don't get any sense of the presence of God" from your worship services. If one of your assumptions says "Our church meets the worship needs of its members and its community," obviously, there is a *problem* to be faced. It should be listed on your newsprint as a major *area of concern* requiring attention.

Suppose, further, another of your assumptions states, "The best hour for worship is at 11:00 A.M. on Sunday morning." Your Information Summary says that some of your members are infirm and do not leave home for any reason. The summary also shows that a number of church families spend weekends at recreation centers. If your data are true, you will have been acting on incorrect assumptions. This is a good reason why worship should be considered an *area of concern* by the congregation.

A Fellowship Example

Now suppose your church purpose statement says, "God wants us to live together in fellowship as His family." From your Information Summary you know that several church members (and even more persons in the church's neighborhood) go for months without any meaningful visits or fellowship. You also find your church has not provided small groups where individuals or couples can get together on their own for prayer and Bible study, for social hours after services, for work projects, or for special events. Yet, one of your theological assumptions says "God calls us to love one another." You have identified an obvious *problem* which is also a *challenge* and an *opportunity;* list it as a major *area of concern.*

A Mission Example

Suppose, further, that your purpose statement says, "Our Lord, Jesus Christ, has charged us to go into the world to preach, to teach, to heal, and to help." But your Information Summary tells you few members know what your church is doing in evangelism and social action; in fact, they know so little they cannot say whether they agree or disagree with it. Two of your theological assumptions state, "Jesus Christ, God's Son, died for our sins to establish fellowship between us and God," and, "God wants us to be involved in the world's healing." Note the tension between these theological assumptions and the Information Summary. The *issue* of your congregation's lack of mission awareness should be listed as a major *area of concern* for your Planning Task Force.

An Education Example

Further, your Information Summary shows many members say they do not know what they believe well enough to share their faith with others. One of your operational assumptions states: "Our current church school program fails to prepare our members for mission." An education and training *problem* should be added to your list as an *area of concern.*

The four examples given above suggest a style for identifying and defining your Areas of Concern. Other concerns will emerge as you study your assumption lists and Information Summary. In Step 2:8 your task will be to write goals which guide you in responding to these concerns.

———————

Now, if back on page 35 you elected to use **Option #1** for your reporting style, your Areas of Concern can be placed in the categories that will be used for examples throughout the rest of this *Manual.* If you elected to use **Option #2,** or some other reporting style, you will need to create your own categories for your Areas of Concern. Your categories can then be compared with the ones used as illustrations.

To review, **Option #1** categories are:

A. Developing spiritually vital church members.

B. Expanding educational ministries.

C. Performing Christ's work in the community.

D. Sharing Christ with unbelievers.

E. Extending our mission throughout the world.

F. Making our church life more productive and efficient through improved operations.

Put six sheets of newsprint on the wall. At the top of each sheet write one of the above six categories, A through F, or use your own categories. Draw a vertical line down the middle of each newsprint sheet. To the left of the line write the issues, problems, opportunities/challenges, or needs you have identified. To the right of the line, list the related Area(s) of Concern you have identified.

Illustration:

A. DEVELOPING SPIRITUALLY VITAL CHURCH MEMBERS	
INFORMATION	**CONCERN**
Church attendance is down Many members are inactive Lack of enthusiasm A few people are doing all the work Difficulty raising budget	Inactive church members

Some examples are given below to show how Areas of Concern can be fitted into one or another of the six categories A through F. Only one piece of information and one related concern are listed for each example. Your actual list will probably include many pieces of information and a number of concerns related to each category. *EXAMPLES:*

Category A. Developing spiritually vital church members.
　　　　　　—*Information:* Many of our church members are inactive. (This could identify a problem, define a need or an opportunity.)
　　　　　　—*Concern:*　　Inactive church members

Category B. Expanding educational ministries.
　　　　　　—*Information:* Church school attendance is down 8 percent from last year.
　　　　　　—*Concern:*　　Decline in church school attendance.

Category C. Performing Christ's work in the community.
　　　　　　—*Information:* None of our members serve on a community board or committee.
　　　　　　—*Concern:*　　Lack of Christian influence in community affairs.

Category D. Sharing Christ with unbelievers.
　　　　　　—*Information:* Few of our church members are witnessing Christians.
　　　　　　—*Concern:*　　Lack of witnessing Christians.

Category E. Extending our mission throughout the world.
　　　　　　—*Information:* World hunger is an increasing crisis.
　　　　　　—*Concern:*　　Thousands of persons around the world are starving.

Category F. Making our church life more productive and efficient through improved operations.
　　　　　　—*Information:* Our old furnace is using more fuel than two years ago.
　　　　　　—*Concern:*　　It costs too much to heat our building.

Look for an order of priority emerging among the Areas of Concern you have listed. Identify the Areas you feel should receive immediate attention.

Place a "1" next to those Areas of Concern you feel need top priority attention. Do not limit yourself necessarily to one "1"; perhaps several of your concerns will require quick attention. Then, place a "2," "3," "4," etc., after each remaining item to indicate what you feel is its level of urgency.

If more than one Area of Concern receives a "1" priority, consider each of these concerns until you have been able to choose what you feel is the *number one Area of Concern for your church* and have placed the others in priority order beneath it. Use fresh newsprint to copy your Areas of Concern in priority order.

Getting Ready for Step 2:8

The Planning Task Force chairperson should, before the next meeting, make arrangements to have available the materials and resources necessary for writing goal statements. These would include your *Areas of Concern* in priority order, your *assumption* lists, your *Information Summary,* and the *Purpose Statement* of your church.

Have an ample supply of newsprint available for Step 2:8 .

Both the Old and New Testaments provide many illustrations of goals. Begin your session on Step 2:8 with a devotional centered on one of these. Ask God's guidance as you work on your goals.

Stating Goals

Planning is based on a continuous movement from purpose to goals.

PURPOSE → GOALS

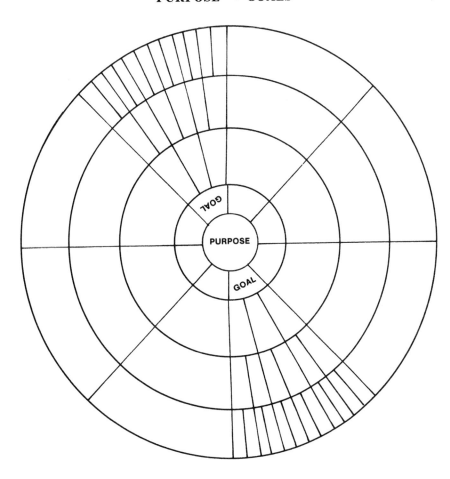

WRITE GOALS

STEP 2:8

A goal expresses *a condition or "end-state" you wish to attain.*[10] It should be rooted in the purpose of your congregation and should always reflect your Purpose Statement.

Your church's goals should be easily understood by your members and should express their desired long-range results of ministry. Including your members' desires in your planning helps your goals come alive and have meaning.

Each goal should focus on what your major accomplishments in mission ought to be in light of your church's purpose. Church goals must be "owned" if they are, in fact, to focus your congregation's attention and resources (its time, personnel, finances, and facilities).

Goal statements, when correctly written, do not mention program details or any "how to" steps. Means and methods for pursuing goals are dealt with later in the planning process.

Some aids for writing vital goal statements:

1. *Be clear in what you say.* Avoid jargon or unfamiliar theological words or phrases.
2. *Have one point (or focus) for each goal statement.* If your goal has more than one main point, use more than one goal statement.
3. *Be sure your goal statement says only what the final result (end-state) will be, not how you will reach it.* Do not include what you will do to achieve your goal. Program plans, time frames, program costs, who will perform certain tasks, etc., are dealt with later.
4. *Be concise.* State *briefly* what the end-state or condition will be.
5. *Make the goal statement challenging and realistic,* neither so easy that people will not be motivated, nor so gigantic as to produce frustration.
6. *Goal statements should reflect your purpose statement.* In other words, they should point to or be rooted in a concept in your purpose statement.
7. Keep in mind that *your members will need to "buy in" to each goal.* You will need their support if it is to be accomplished.

AN EXERCISE

To test your understanding of what a goal should be, read the following illustration and try your hand at writing a goal statement related to it.

Suppose on a warm and sunny day you arrive at the shore of a beautiful lake. You hear that across the lake, beyond reach by car, is a scenic waterfall. To see this sight, one must go to the other side of the lake. You decide to see the waterfall. After making some inquiries, you discover there are rowboats, canoes, and motorboats for rent. Upon further checking, you find that an excursion boat crosses the lake at frequent intervals. Besides all these possibilities, you are a good swimmer and happen to have your bathing suit along!

What would be your goal in this situation? Read the story again if necessary. Write your goal statement below:

---

[10] Perhaps the most misused term in the planning process is the word "goal." Many persons confuse program plans or objectives with goals. See the definitions of these terms in the front of the book.

Now check what you have written. Does your statement contain anything about your need to get to the other side of the lake? Does it say anything about the means of transportation for crossing the lake? It shouldn't.

The goal from this short story is simply, "To view the waterfall." Such a goal is short, concise, and to the point.

It might appear, at first, that your goal would be to get to the other side of the lake. Getting to the other side, however, as well as the way used to get there are means (program plans)[11] employed *in order to view the waterfall*. The goal statement itself should include nothing about means (how you are going to get there, how much it will cost, how much time it will take, etc.). The goal statement should indicate only the end result you seek.

TYPES OF GOAL STATEMENTS

Goal statements fit either of two types: *one type* covers goals which reflect the church's total mission, goals common to all members of the congregation; *the other type* covers goals pointing to a particular group, age level, or area of interest. A total mission goal might reflect the intentions of all members of your congregation about the Sunday morning worship service. A particular goal might deal with the needs of your church's youth in the morning worship service.

WHO SHOULD PARTICIPATE IN WRITING GOALS

It is helpful and proper to involve persons beyond the Planning Task Force in goal writing, especially persons who will be directly affected. Some benefits of involving others are:
1. It broadens participation in church planning.
2. More persons will know that goal statements are being developed.
3. It can provide additional input, and perhaps, resources.
4. There will be greater understanding of what the goal statements mean.
5. More persons will tend to "own" the goals created in this fashion.

Involve as many people as possible in creating the church's goal statements.

---

[11] Remember, program plans are treated later in this planning process.

This planning manual offers three options for involving others in writing goals (and objectives).[12] The basic concept is that your *Planning Task Force cannot and should not, on its own, try to write the congregation's goals* and then expect church members to "buy in" and support them. Try to involve others in writing goal statements *at the level of their interest or elected responsibility.* Your pastor should be present at each goal writing session. You may also want to invite your area minister or another consultant to work with you as you write your goals.

Option #1

Many churches have committees, task forces, or boards whose work fits within the categories listed on page 45. If your church is organized in this way, then you already have a list of leaders whom you should involve in writing goal statements. For example:

Category A: *Developing spiritually vital church members.*
Church council
Diaconate
Nurture commission
Spiritual committee
Worship committee

Category B: *Expanding educational ministries.*
Representatives of each age level
Board or commission of Christian education
Church school superintendent
Education specialists or volunteers

Category C: *Performing Christ's work in the community.*
Age level organizations
Diaconate
Outreach committee
Small-group representatives
Social concerns committee

Category D: *Sharing Christ with unbelievers.*
Diaconate
Evangelism committee
Outreach committee
Witness commission

Category E: *Extending our mission throughout the world.*
Committee or board of missions
School of missions chairperson
Small groups (women's organization, etc.)

Category F: *Making our church life more productive and efficient through improved operations.*
Board of trustees
Pastoral relations committee
Personnel committee

---

[12] Whether you choose Option #1 or Option #2, a further choice is to begin writing *objectives* during the same session at which you are working on *goal statements.* This can be done if you handle only one or two Areas of Concern at each of your goal-writing sessions and use only a little time to write the goal statements. If you choose to work on goals and objectives at the same time, read and study Step 2:9 (Write Objectives) well ahead of time to make the best use of the hours your goal-writing group(s) is/are together.

When many are involved in goal writing, a number of sessions will probably be needed to get the job done. Get one or more representatives from each group in advance of your scheduled goal-writing sessions to ensure maximum participation.

Option #2

The membership of your Planning Task Force may include representatives from all church boards and committees. These persons can serve as communicators between the groups they represent and the Planning Task Force. In this option the Planning Task Force studies its Areas of Concerns and defines possible goals. This work can then be communicated to each board or committee. Each board or committee, in turn, will study the task force's work, possibly revise it, and send it back. Once the Planning Task Force receives the full review and is satisfied with the revisions, it can return the goal statement(s) to the committees and boards for a final check before they are given to the congregation (or official board) for study and action.

Option #3

Another option would be for the Planning Task Force to share with each board or committee the Areas of Concern (and related background material) from   Step 2:7 . Each group would be asked to analyze the material and suggest possible goals. The results could then come to the Planning Task Force for refinement. After this, the refined goal statements would be returned to each board or committee for a final review before being given to the congregation.

GETTING PERSONS READY TO WRITE GOAL STATEMENTS

Any persons who join you to write goals should be given the background materials the Planning Task Force chairperson gathered according to the instructions on page 47. Take time to acquaint them with what was done in   Step 2:7 . Don't rush through this important orientation. Help them understand what led you to identify each Area of Concern. This is important since *each* goal should reflect a *major* Area of Concern you have identified. Each Area of Concern implies one goal. Display the newsprint from   Step 2:7   on which you listed your concerns in priority order.

WRITING YOUR GOAL STATEMENTS

By this point, you should have: (1) studied the definitions and the principles about goal statements; (2) used the exercise on pages 48-49; (3) decided which option to follow to involve others; (4) prepared other persons to work with you. Now, write your goal statements by taking each Area of Concern in priority order.

As you write, don't hesitate to strike out words or phrases or add suggestions made by the group. Write a goal all over again when necessary. When the writing group has agreed on a goal statement, write it on a clean sheet of newsprint and move on to another Area of Concern.

Some Planning Task Forces or writing groups will want to schedule no more than two goal-writing sessions each month. Such timing can actually benefit your goal-writing process, since reports back to the parent body will provide a *flow* of information rather than a *flood,* which happens when many goals (and their related objectives) are presented at one time. Determine the pace that is best for your church.

Some Examples

Here are several examples of goal statements for the categories used to illustrate the mission of your church.

Category A: Developing spiritually vital church members.

Area of Concern: Inactive church members

Goal: A majority of our members will be active in the mission of our church.

Illustration:

A. Developing Spiritually Vital Church Members	
Concern Inactive church members	**Goal** A majority of our members will be active in the mission of our church.

Category B: Expanding educational ministries.

Area of Concern: A decline in church school attendance

Goal: The number of persons participating in the Christian education experiences of our church will be increased.

Category C: Performing Christ's work in the community.

Area of Concern: Lack of Christian influence in community affairs

Goal: Our surrounding community will be influenced by our expressing as a congregation an "evangelistic life-style."

Category D: Sharing Christ with unbelievers.

Area of Concern: Lack of witnessing Christians

Goal: We will be a witnessing congregation.

Category E: Extending our mission throughout the world.

Area of Concern: Thousands of persons around the world are starving.

Goal: Persons, who without our help would starve, will be fed.

Category F: Making our church life more productive and efficient through improved operations.

Area of Concern: It costs too much to heat our building.

Goal: Maximum comfort at minimum cost will be provided for persons taking part in activities in our church building.

TEST YOUR GOAL STATEMENTS

Ask five questions about each of your goal statements:

1. *Does the goal statement say anything?*

    If it does, does it speak clearly? Some goal statements sound very impressive and attractive but mean something different to each reader. Does your statement mean about the same thing to each person who reads it?

2. *Is the goal attainable by your church?*

    If the goal, as stated, is obviously impossible for your church to accomplish, revise the statement until your members feel they can make reasonable progress toward it.

3. *Does the goal reflect the Purpose Statement of your church?*
Be able to identify which part of your Purpose Statement covers, implies, or is related to each goal.

4. *Will your membership "own" the goal?*
"Ownership" by your members is imperative. Will work toward this goal receive reasonable support from your congregation?

5. *Does the goal statement point only to one desired end-state?*
Be sure the goal statement has only one focus and does not say anything about how you will reach the end-state.

Then, ask one more question.

How completely do your goal statements, when considered together, cover what is implied by your statement of purpose?

Check to see what areas of your Purpose Statement are not touched by the goals you have defined.

Setting Objectives

Planning is based on a continuous movement from purpose to goals; from goals to their related objectives.

PURPOSE ⟶ GOALS ⟶ OBJECTIVES

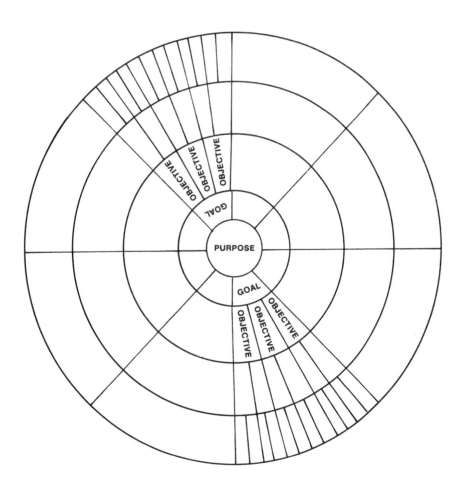

WRITE OBJECTIVES

An objective is *a clear, simple statement of a target to be reached.* It is derived from a goal statement. Usually you will be able to identify several objectives for each goal. (See the above diagram.) As an example, one group wrote sixteen objectives for the same goal. Each of the sixteen expressed a distinct part of that goal.

Objectives can be classified by the time period needed to achieve them. *Short-term* objectives imply time periods of two years or less; *long-term* objectives refer to time periods of more than two years. Many planners feel that five-year time blocks set a good range for long-term objectives. Except in unusual circumstances, program planners seldom try to project beyond a ten- to fifteen-year period.

An objective should be stated so its achievement can be measured, in order to test movement toward the goal to which it is related. To determine if the objective can be measured, answer such questions as these:

—Who, or what persons, are to be involved or helped?
—How many? How much?
—Where?
—When? (Beginning when? Accomplished when?)

A good objective statement has one verb implying a specific action, such as *write, interview, organize, invite, vote, build, tutor, design,* etc. Avoid vague or general action verbs, such as *understand, serve, grow,* etc. Check Appendix J for five principles to use in choosing the verb for each objective.

A good objective statement is a target to be reached. It has an action verb.

WRITE
ORGANIZE
BUILD

Sample objectives worksheets, using the categories and goals identified earlier on pages 51 and 52, are given below as they would be written on newsprint.

OBJECTIVES WORKSHEET

Category A: Developing spiritually vital church members

Area of Concern: Inactive church members

Goal: A majority of our members will be active in the mission of our church.

Objectives: —Within two months, our congregation will officially adopt a common definition for the terms "active members" and "inactive members."   ST*

—Within two months after our congregation adopts the definitions, each church member will be placed on either an active member or inactive member list.   ST*

—Within three months, our congregation will approve at least two new plans to involve our inactive members in the life and ministry of our church.   ST*

—Within three years from the time we begin to carry out the new plans to involve inactive members, we will have 30 percent of them involved in our church mission. LT**

---

*Short Term
**Long Term

Comment: Obviously, several more objectives could be written for this goal statement and for the others listed below as examples. Do not limit your thinking to three or four objectives for each goal. Include as many objectives as you can. Later, you will decide which objectives best fit your church. Meanwhile, "the sky's the limit."

OBJECTIVES WORKSHEET

Category B: Expanding educational ministries

Area of Concern: A decline in church school attendance

Goal: The number of persons participating in the Christian education experiences of our church will be increased.

Objectives: —Within the next sixty days, find out if our church school can grow in numbers.   ST

—Within the next six months, create one new educational study opportunity for adults.   ST

—Increase our church school attendance by 10 percent within twelve months of *(give date)*.   ST

—Within three years, provide regular training for our teachers in which at least 90 percent participate.   LT

Illustration: The Plymouth Valley Baptist Church near Norristown, Pennsylvania, was experiencing a serious decline in its church school. Average attendance was sixty persons. The church felt it could do better. In a goal and objective writing session, the Board of Christian Education wrote a short-term growth objective.

". . . within eighteen months, we will increase our average church school attendance from 60 to 100 persons per Sunday."

They designed program plans to carry out the objective. Less than one year later church school average attendance was 102 persons per Sunday. The accomplishment of this objective was celebrated by the church during a morning worship service!

OBJECTIVES WORKSHEET

Category C: Performing Christ's work in the community

Area of Concern: Lack of Christian influence in
community affairs

Goal: Our surrounding community will be influenced by our
expressing as a congregation an "evangelistic life style."

Objectives: —Within twelve months help at least one community group to examine theologically what it is doing.   ST
—Within the next three years, talk with every major community agency and institution to identify the needs of our community.   LT

OBJECTIVES WORKSHEET

Category D: Sharing Christ with unbelievers

Area of Concern: Lack of witnessing Christians

Goal: We will be a witnessing congregation.

Objectives: —Within sixty days have at least 50 percent of our congregation know the basis of an Evangelistic Life Style and be able to name the seven marks that identify it.[13]
                     ST
—Enlist 10 percent of our congregation in a new program of community witness during the next year.   ST
—Enlist 20 percent of our membership each year to develop skills for person-to-person witness.   ST
—Within the next three years develop a master plan for community witness involving 60 percent of our membership.

---

[13] The Evangelistic Life Style and its seven marks are described in *Becoming Good News People*, edited by Richard M. Jones (Valley Forge: Board of National Ministries, American Baptist Churches in the U.S.A., 1974).

OBJECTIVES WORKSHEET

Category E: Extending our mission through the world

Area of Concern: Thousands of persons around the world
are starving.

Goal: Persons, who without our help would starve, will be fed.

Objectives: —Within three months we will raise $1,000 to send food to an
area of identified need.   ST
—Within two months, we will secure a commitment from our
congressional representative to support the release of
additional U.S. grain supplies to countries where persons
are starving.   ST
—Within the next three months, we will find out what our
denomination is doing in response to the world hunger
problem.   ST
—We will increase our giving to our denomination's mission
budget by 25 percent in the next three years.   LT

OBJECTIVES WORKSHEET

Category F: Making our church life more productive and
efficient through improved operations

Area of Concern: It costs too much to heat our building.

Goal: Maximum comfort at minimum cost will be provided for
persons taking part in activities in our church building.

Objectives: —Within six months, decide how to cut costs in heating our
building.   ST
—Within three years reduce our heating costs by 10 percent.
LT

Comment: Remember, these examples of goal-oriented objectives are only *samples* of what could be written.

The Planning Task Force should begin writing objectives by selecting the goal statement related to the first Area of Concern. Describe some specifics that will help to achieve a part of what the goal states. Be careful *not* to include in objective statements any "how to" (the methods or program plans that might be used to reach the objective).

Study your goal statements and write down all related objectives that occur to you. Do not limit yourself. Later in the planning process there will be time for comparing the objectives to choose which ones your church will use. Use newsprint and follow the style you used to develop your goal statements. (See page 55.)

GETTING YOUR OBJECTIVES READY FOR USE IN EVALUATION

You read on page 54 that an objective is derived from a goal statement (a desired long-range result of ministry). You also read that an objective should be written so its achievement can be measured. These ideas point to the reasons for objectives. Planners write objectives in order to divide a goal into pieces which: (1) can be handled within a reasonable time period (ranging from a few weeks to two years or so) and (2) can be handled so you know what is being accomplished. Well-stated objectives, then, have at least two specific uses:

1. A well-stated objective sharpens the focus for *action*. It increases the possibility of developing program plans and program plan details (see Phase III) that will work in your church's situation.
2. A well-stated objective sharpens the focus for *reflection*. It helps you to decide how well your program plan moved toward what was intended and how you can improve future program plans.

Reflection involves "evaluation." In this *Manual* evaluation is dealt with fully in Phase V. However, it is important here to introduce a few evaluation ideas:

- An objective states what a planner intends or expects to result from what is done.
- Evaluation involves deciding how well you accomplished what was expected or intended when you wrote your objective.
- Such expectations or intentions imply *clues* or *signs,* called criteria.
- A good objective statement will point to its criteria—what the planner should look for, observe, count, or measure in some way as a basis for evaluation.

The *criteria* implied by a stated objective (that is, the clues or signs) are evidence which provide a way of checking how much of the objective has been achieved and how well the program plan helped in the achievement.

Defining criteria for each objective points to things which two or more observers can see, taste, touch, smell, hear, or at least be aware of in some conscious way. As always, "beauty is in the eye of the beholder." However, by setting criteria, you make it possible for two or more persons to agree on the clues or signs of "beauty" and on how much "beauty" is present in a given instance.

The marks of good clues or signs (criteria) are:

1. Each must be valid—that is, it must be a faithful measure for that objective.
2. Each must be reliable—that is, it must measure similar things in the same way each time it is used.
3. Each must be reasonable in cost—that is, it must not be too expensive to use (to observe and to record).
4. Each must be legitimate—that is, it must respect the individual's right for privacy.

At this point take each objective as you have stated it and decide what measurable criteria (clues or signs) you will use. Include these criteria in an indented paragraph under each of your stated objectives.

We illustrate some criteria by using the first objective in Category A.

OBJECTIVES WORKSHEET

Category A: Developing spiritually vital church members

Area of Concern: Inactive church members

Goal: A majority of our members will be active in the mission of our church.

Objective: —Within two months, our congregation will officially adopt a common definition for the terms "active members" and "inactive members."   ST

Criteria:
- One church group has carried full responsibility for developing the definitions and bringing these to the congregation for action.
- The objective was achieved within the eight-week period set for it.
- The members of the congregation, before voting on the definitions, had at least two opportunities, as required by our bylaws, to become familiar with the definitions and how they would be used.
- The minutes of church board, committee, commission meetings show that the definitions were discussed in such elected bodies before the congregation was asked to vote.
- The official minutes of the church carry a record of the congregation's favorable vote on the definitions and their use.

Objective: —Within two months after our congregation adopts the definitions, each church member will be placed on either an active member or inactive member list.   ST

Criteria:

<table>
<tr><td>STEP
2:10</td></tr>
</table>

SET PRIORITIES AMONG OBJECTIVES

Begin this step with a Bible study. Read 1 Peter 2:9-21. Discuss what it means to be God's own people. Close your Bible study with prayer asking God's help in setting priorities among your objectives.

From Step 2:7 your goal statements are in order according to the priorities you set among your Areas of Concern.

If you are like most Planning Task Forces, you have probably written more objectives for each goal than your congregation can work on at one time. Use the guidelines given below to examine each objectives worksheet. Mark each objective with the number of each guideline that applies. For example, objectives which fit the foundation guideline should be marked with a "2."

GUIDELINES FOR PUTTING OBJECTIVES INTO PRIORITY ORDER

1. *Objectives Based on What the Bible Is Saying to Your Congregation*

   In Step 2:6 you listed your church's biblical and theological

What does the Bible say to us about priorities?

assumptions. Study that list again. What should your church be doing in light of your biblical and theological assumptions? Does the way you have declared the mission of your church require that certain functions be carried out, e.g., evangelism, ministry to others, etc.?

2. *Foundation Objectives*

The statement "We must achieve this objective if we are to be in a position to minister to others" illustrates foundation objectives. "To have a pastor, we must pay a living salary." "To use a church building, we must maintain it." Not to achieve foundation objectives means you simply can't continue to serve as an organized congregation.

3. *What's Near Your Church Doorstep?*

Certain special needs may exist in the community immediately surrounding your church property. What can you do to respond to them? What are the opportunities for service God has put on your doorstep?

4. *Ready Resources*

Can the objective be met rather easily because the congregation already has available to it special resources, skills, talents, time, and facilities? To illustrate, a church located near a city once had several members who owned farms. Many children in a nearby inner city usually had only the city streets for play for the summer. A ready resource (the members who owned farms with "soil banked" land) made it relatively easy to accomplish the objective: "Get fifty city children into the fresh air next summer." Day camping on some of the soil bank acreage of church members' farms was soon a reality.

5. *What Is Your Church Doing Right Now?*

Some objectives may reflect programs already under way. It isn't necessary to stop such programs just because you have begun a planning process. If a new objective covers things you are presently doing, relate what is being done to the objective in each of the next phases of planning.

6. *Finances*

Funds may appear available to achieve an objective or could be made available if the program plan included fund raising in it.

7. *What Has Your Church Been Asked to Do?*

During interviews with community agencies and organizations did any of them ask your church to take responsibility for specific projects? Does the objective reflect things your community has asked you to do?

Are we listening to what the community is telling us?

8. *What's "In"?*

Does the objective focus on issues or areas of concern about which your people are already enthusiastic and eager to do something, *right now?* Sometimes a short-term objective should be undertaken immediately to benefit from enthusiasm about what is crucial at the moment.

9. *What's Going On in Your Denomination?*

Does the objective reflect any priorities you have heard about from your denomination? Perhaps your congregation should consider working on objectives being highlighted or suggested within its larger family.

10. *How Clear Are Your Criteria?*

A good objective suggests its criteria—what the planner should look for, observe, count, or measure in some way as a basis for evaluation. (See page 58). Does the objective point to criteria? Do you know what to look for as evidence that the change required by the objective has really taken place?

COMPLETING THE STEP OF SETTING PRIORITIES

When you have completed the task of testing all your objectives against these guidelines, each objective may have one or more guideline numbers written next to it. For each objective count how many guideline numbers it has and write the count in the right-hand margin of the newsprint. Within each goal put the objectives in priority order according to the count each received. When a tie occurs, put the objective having more of the first three guideline numbers ahead of the other(s).

Bring each goal, with its related objectives in priority order, to the congregation for approval. Ask the congregation to approve the *goals,* using the objectives only as illustrations of what the goals imply. Actual objectives will be developed later.

Display your goals and objectives in your sanctuary and educational facilities where they may be seen easily. Put them in your church bulletins, newsletters, and other media. Later, when your church accomplishes an objective, celebrate the occasion.

Preparation for Mission Design

First . . . *TAKE A BREAK!* Your Planning Task Force has just spent important time and energy completing Goal Development. Schedule no task force meetings for at least three weeks. Relax!

Second . . . During these weeks check with Planning Task Force members to see who will be able to continue to serve. You may need to replace some members. Now is a good time to bring replacements "on board" if they are needed.

The next diagram shows where you are in the planning process.

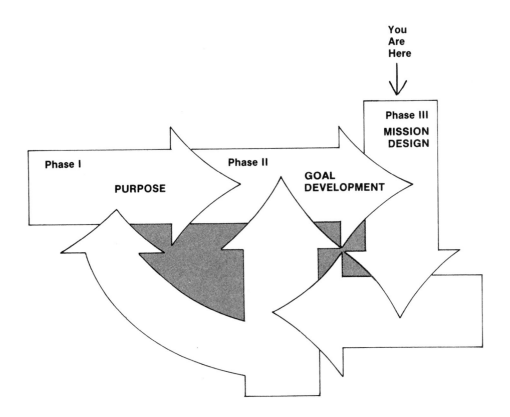

Building Program Plans

Planning is based on a continuous movement from purpose to goals; from goals to their related objectives; from objectives to their program plans.

PURPOSE ──▶ GOALS ──▶ OBJECTIVES ──▶ PROGRAM PLANS

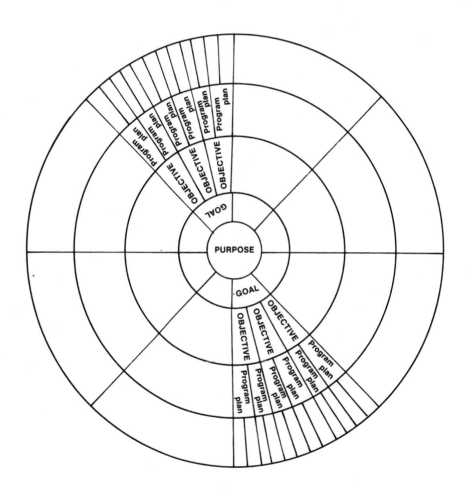

Phase III
Mission Design

STEP
3:0

INTRODUCTION

You have now stated your Goals and their related priority Objectives. Objectives, however, don't just happen. Your task now is to design ways your church can best work to achieve its objectives.

A clearly defined objective will suggest a number of ways to reach it. We call these ways or methods *Program Plans* (some persons use the term "strategies"). Program Plans give you opportunities to work out new ways to get things done.

After you have created your *Program Plans*, the next step in Mission Design will be to develop *Program Plan Details* for each one.

STEP
3:1

PROGRAM PLANS

A Program Plan is *an overall blueprint describing in general how to use what you have to achieve each objective.* Most of your objectives can be achieved in a number of ways. Current ways of getting things done in your church may not always make the best use of your resources. This step involves picking the most promising way of reaching the objective for which you can prepare a blueprint.

The overall blueprint is a plan of action to help our church grow from where it is to where it should be.

In Step 3:1 you should explore as many ways as you can to work toward each objective. Look over these questions as you begin to develop Program Plans:

1. Who is the target audience?
   a. For whom is this objective intended?
   b. Who would be served by this objective if it were achieved?
2. Can we organize our congregation to reach this objective?
   a. Do we really have the "horses needed to pull this wagon"?
   b. What advance arrangements would we have to make if we decide to use this particular blueprint or Program Plan?
   c. Should we try to do this work by ourselves? Will we have to get help from some other group? If so, what kind and how much?
3. Can we motivate our church members to achieve this objective?
   a. Are we motivated to do what the objective challenges us to do?
   b. Will our congregation risk what is required by this objective?

Remember, each Program Plan describes *in general* a course of action that could be taken to reach a priority objective. A Program Plan indicates:

> (1) principal actors (congregation, boards, committees, task forces);
> (2) particular responsibilities; and (3) the types of human and financial resources needed to carry out the action.

Some objectives may be so specific they indicate only one way that can be used to work toward them. If this is the case with any of your objectives, don't waste time trying to generate other possibilities just for the sake of having more than one Program Plan to consider. Begin to develop Program Plans for the objectives you ranked as *most important* in Step 2:10 of Goal Development.

WHO SHOULD DEVELOP PROGRAM PLANS

Here are three options for who should be involved in generating ideas for Program Plans.

Option 1. The Planning Task Force can work alone. However, others in the church may feel left out of the process.

Option 2. Identify the particular Program Plan categories the Planning Task Force hopes to cover at its next meeting. Invite to that meeting persons from boards, committees, or age groups related to categories you will discuss. Include them in your process.

Option 3. For each objective invite the board, committee, or other organized unit of the church which best fits the subject of that objective to develop the related Program Plan. The Planning Task Force's job would be to coordinate the development of all Program Plans. If a unit is not represented on the Planning Task Force, a task force member could be asked to work with the unit while it is developing the Program Plan.

Your community probably has resource persons, such as area ministers, other denominational staff persons, seminary and university faculty, local community organizers, etc. These persons can help you expand the number of your Program Plan possibilities. They can assist you under any of the three options.

HOW TO DEVELOP PROGRAM PLANS

Write one objective statement at the top of each sheet of newsprint. Brainstorm for five to fifteen minutes possible ways to achieve the objective. Encourage your people to say what pops into their minds for each objective. Be open and creative.

Don't stop to analyze any of the suggested ideas or to discuss details. Let the ideas flow. Be different. Be daring.

Write on newsprint every idea, dream, and hope that your group suggests. Don't limit yourself because of high costs, lack of staff, or lack of facilities. Don't hesitate to suggest what might, at first, appear to be "way out" ideas.

At the conclusion of your brainstorming session you will probably have many ideas on the newsprint sheets. Sort out the ideas you feel are most meaningful and usable for your church and community. Try combining some ideas to build a Program Plan. Work with various combinations of ideas until a plan emerges about which the group can be enthusiastic.

A word of caution. You may have difficulty listing Program Plan ideas for certain objectives. If this happens, there are three things you can do:

1. You can assign to someone the job of developing a Program Plan. This work could then be brought back to the group for reaction.
2. You might contact denominational staff for suggestions.
3. You may have to set aside an objective if, after some exploration, there seems to be no possible way for your church to pursue it.

EXAMPLES OF PROGRAM PLANS

The following examples use the categories and objectives presented earlier on pages 55 through 57.

Category A: Developing spiritually vital church members.
    Objective: Short Term—Within two months, our congregation will officially adopt a common definition for the terms "active members" and "inactive members."
    Program Plan: Ask the diaconate to define terms and get the congregation to vote on them.

Category B: Expanding educational ministries.
    Objective: Short Term—Within the next sixty days find out if our church school can grow in numbers.
    Program Plan: Have a task force study and report the potential for each age group to be reached by our church school.

Category C: Performing Christ's work in the community.
    Objective: Long Term—Within the next three years, talk with every community agency and institution to identify the needs of our community.
    Program Plan: The Committee on Evangelism and the Committee on Social Concern will jointly prepare a procedure to talk with community agencies and institutions to find out their perceptions of our community needs.

Category D: Sharing Christ with unbelievers.
    Objective: Short Term—Within sixty days have at least 50 percent of our congregation know the basis of an Evangelistic Life Style and be able to name the seven marks that identify it.
    Program Plan: Interpret the Evangelistic Life Style emphasis to our congregation during the next sixty days by holding a special service to introduce the emphasis to our congregation.

Category E: Extending our mission throughout the world.
    Objective: Short Term—Within three months we will raise $1,000

to send food to an area of identified need.

Program Plan: In this ninety-day period the congregation will hold a series of fund-raising events to raise $1,000.

Category F: *Making our church life more productive and efficient through improved operations.*

Objective: Short Term—Within six months decide how to cut costs in heating our building.

Program Plan: The Board of Trustees will study our building heating plant and the way we use our building to recommend ways to cut costs. These recommendations will be given to the congregation for review and approval.

Outlining Program Plan Details

Planning is based on a continuous movement from purpose to goals; from goals to their related objectives; from objectives to their program plans; from program plans to their program plan details.

PURPOSE ──▶ GOALS ──▶ OBJECTIVES ──▶ PROGRAM PLANS ──▶ PROGRAM PLAN DETAILS

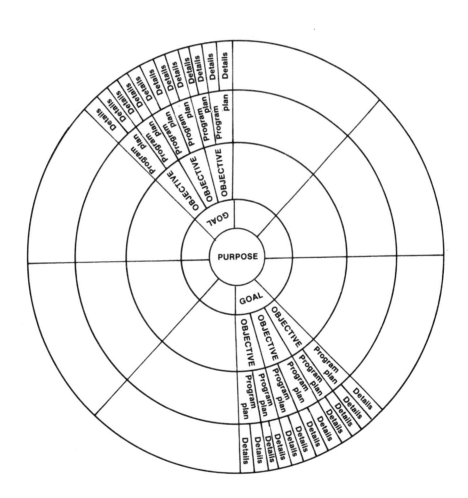

<table>
<tr><td>

STEP
3:2

</td></tr>
</table>

PREPARING PROGRAM PLAN DETAILS

Individual parts of a Program Plan are called Program Plan Details. The following questions will help you identify what should be included as details of a Program Plan:

1. *What* is the *Objective* and its related *Program Plan?*
2. *Who* will be involved in making this happen?
3. *When* will this happen?
   (When will the events of the program begin?
   When will they be finished?)
4. *Where* will this happen?
   (And, under what conditions?)
5. *How* will this happen?
   (What will persons *do* to make this happen?)
6. *What* specifically *will be different or changed* if what happens is successful?
   (Be sure to relate this to your criteria. See pages 58-59.)

Program Plan Details provide a complete description of: (1) what is to be done; (2) who will be involved; (3) what their specific assignments are; (4) the target dates when their work will begin and be completed, and the dates when progress reports are to be made; and (5) the changes that are intended.

Think of a Program Plan as an architect's sketches and pictures. Consider Program Plan Details as the blueprints which explain just how to build. They show everyone involved exactly what to do and when.

A building project requires a detailed set of blueprints and a construction schedule. In the same way program planning requires specific descriptions of activities and a schedule for doing what is planned.

When you are ready to work on Program Plan Details, decide first *who* will be the Program Plan Manager.[1] Invite this person to develop the Program Plan Details for review by the Planning Task Force. The best Program Plan can fail if the leaders responsible for it do not understand it or are not committed to it. Having the leaders develop the Program Plan Details is a good way to avoid later misunderstandings or a lack of commitment.

Program Plan Managers should consider these guidelines when working out their Program Plan Details:

1. Be realistic about the time your church will need to carry out the details of a Program Plan.
2. Maintain direct communications with others who will be involved in carrying out the Program Plan Details.
3. Be realistic about the dollars required by each detail of the Program Plan, including both direct and hidden costs.
4. Create a blueprint, the detailed guidelines to help you carry out the plan.
5. Be careful not to skip details. Double-check each one.
6. Provide guidance for any others sharing in your Program Plan Details to know where to get help if they need it.
7. Plan to collect evaluation facts as you go along so you can measure your progress during and at the conclusion of the Program Plan. Refer to Phase V, Step 5:2 for the tools needed to collect your facts.
8. Decide how often you will compare your evaluation facts with the Objective to

[1] See STEP 4:1 , Program Plan Manager, on pages 79-80.

see if the Program Plan Details are doing what they were designed to do.

9. Make sure that you as Program Plan Manager know from the start: (1) when to make both progress reports and the final evaluation report; and (2) the reporting procedures to be used.

Newsprint can be used when developing your Program Plan Details. Write the Objective at the top of the sheet; then state the Program Plan as written in ⸤Step 3:1⸥.

The following examples use the Categories, Objectives, and Program Plans listed on pages 67 through 68. The details answer the questions found on page 70 and follow the form of the Sample Worksheet shown on page 77.

(Example)

Category A: Developing spiritually vital church members.

1. *Objective: Short Term*—Within two months, our congregation will officially adopt a common definition for the terms "active members" and "inactive members."

    Program Plan: Ask the diaconate to define terms and get the congregation to vote on them.

2. *Who will make this happen?*

    (a) The Program Plan Manager will begin the process by inviting the diaconate to take responsibility for this Program Plan.

    (b) The diaconate will consider the invitation and, if it accepts, will submit its work to the church moderator.

    (c) The church moderator and/or the pastor will call a church business meeting and preside over it.

    (d) The congregation will decide.

3. *When will this happen?*

    The definitions should be ready by (date) . The congregational vote should take place by (date) .

4. *Where will this happen?*

    At the next meeting of the diaconate, to be held at John Smith's home, and at the (date) business meeting of our church.

5. *How will this happen?*

    (a) The diaconate will ask the church clerk to provide copies of church membership policies and church actions about membership for its study.

    (b) The diaconate will prepare its definitions and give them to the church moderator at least two weeks before the church business meeting.

    (c) The church moderator and/or the pastor by (date) will call a congregational meeting to vote on the diaconate's report and will share the proposed definitions at least a week ahead.

    (d) The moderator will preside over the congregational meeting where one hour will be allocated for discussion and/or debate before the vote. Voting will be by secret ballot.

6. *What will be different?*

    We will have a clear distinction between those who are active members and those who are not. We will be able to challenge those now inactive, to inform any who wish to know what is meant by active membership in our church, and to design Program Plans that depend on our knowing just how many active members we have for possible support of the plans.

(Example)

Category B: *Expanding educational ministries.*

1. *Objective: Short Term*—Within the next sixty days find out if our church school can grow in numbers.

   Program Plan: Have a task force study and report the potential for each age group to be reached by our church school.

2. *Who will make this happen?*

   (a) The Program Plan Manager will ask the board of Christian education to authorize a study task force.

   (b) The Program Plan Manager will serve as chairperson of the task force and will appoint its members.

3. *When will this happen?*

   The task force will be named within two weeks.

   The task force will report its work to the board of Christian education by   (date) .

4. *How will this happen?*

   (a) The task force will study the church school and other congregational factors, using the Information Summary prepared by the Planning Task Force.

   (b) The task force will examine community trends and makeup in the study.

   (c) A written report will be presented to the board of Christian education.

5. *Where will this happen?*

   The task force will observe our current use of church school facilities and the community our church school serves.

6. *What will be different?*

   We will *know* what we face in planning our educational ministry for various age groups and will have the necessary information to make decisions about the future of our church school.

(Example)

Category C: *Performing Christ's work in the community.*

1. *Objective: Long Term*—Within the next three years, talk with every community agency and institution to identify the needs of our community.

   Program Plan: The Committee on Evangelism and the Committee on Social Concern will jointly prepare a procedure to talk with community agencies and institutions to find out their perceptions of our community needs.

2. *Who will make this happen?*

   (a) The Program Plan Manager will ask the Committee on Evangelism and the Committee on Social Concern to work together on this study.

(b) The Committee on Evangelism and the Committee on Social Concern, if they agree, will sponsor conversations in the community.

(c) The pastor will train committee members in interviewing techniques (see Appendix H).

(d) Interested community agencies and institutions will talk with our church's representatives.

3. *When will this happen?*

By   (date) , or within six months, the two committees will submit to the church a plan which includes a schedule and a procedure for making reports. The conversations will begin within one year or by   (date) . The completed list of community needs will be reported by   (date) .

4. *How will this happen?*

(a) The Program Plan Manager will ask for time on the next agenda of the two committees to explain the Program Plan and its details.

(b) The Planning Task Force will provide the committees with the Information Summary, along with any other related data they have collected in planning ⌐Step 2:3⌐ .

(c) The two committees, coordinated by the Program Plan Manager, will determine whether they need additional help to carry out the program.

(d) The two committees will compile a list of community agencies, institutions, and organizations to visit.

(e) The two committees will design a systematic plan of visitation and reporting.

(f) The two committees will be trained by the pastor in interviewing before beginning the visits.

(g) The two committees will report on this project one year from now with a review of progress-to-date by   (date) .

5. *Where will this happen?*

Interview meetings will be held in the offices of all community agencies, institutions, and organizations.

6. *What will be different?*

We will have a list of community needs to provide the basis for cooperative action between our church and some community agencies.

(Example)

Category D: Sharing Christ with unbelievers.

1. *Objective: Short Term*—Within sixty days have at least 50 percent of our congregation know the basis of an Evangelistic Life Style and be able to name the seven marks that identify it.

Program Plan: Interpret the Evangelistic Life Style emphasis to our congregation during the next sixty days by holding a special service to introduce the emphasis to our congregation.

2. *Who will make this happen?*

   (a) The Program Plan Manager[2] will enlist the help of the Evangelism Committee.

   (b) The Evangelism Committee will, by next Wednesday, ask for the pastor's cooperation.

   (c) The pastor will lead the preparations for the special service.

3. *When will this happen?*

   (a) A commitment from the Evangelism Committee will be asked by next Sunday.

   (b) A commitment from the pastor will be sought by the following Wednesday.

   (c) A special service will be held no later than   (date)   .

4. *Where will this happen?*

   This special service will take place in our sanctuary at the regular morning worship time.

5. *How will this happen?*

   The Program Plan Manager will provide the Evangelism Committee with the *Evangelistic Life Style Local Congregation Manual.* If it accepts the invitation to sponsor the service, the Evangelism Committee will invite the pastor to act as coordinator, getting any additional persons, resources, and media needed. Publicity for the event will be sent to the congregation through regular channels of communication (newsletter, bulletins, etc.). The Evangelism Committee will arrange with the Church Budget Committee for any needed funds.

6. *What will be different?*

   A large majority of our congregation will have a clear concept of what an Evangelistic Life Style means and of our need to witness to the faith.

(Example)

Category E: *Extending our mission throughout the world.*

1. *Objective: Short Term*—Within three months we will raise $1,000 to send food to an area of identified need.

   Program Plan: In this ninety-day period the congregation will hold a series of fund-raising events to raise $1,000.

2. *Who will make this happen?*

   (a) The Planning Task Force will start the process.

   (b) A special age-level task force will be responsible for the program plan. Its chairperson will be the Program Plan Manager.

   (c) The congregation will create the special task force and approve each proposed fund-raising event.

   (d) The church moderator will call a meeting of the congregation and will receive progress reports.

3. *When will this happen?*

   If the program plan is approved, the special task force will be named

---

[2] The chairperson of the Evangelism Committee will serve as Program Plan Manager.

by (date) . The completion date for raising the $1,000 is (date) .

4. *How will this happen?*

Creating the task force:

(a) The Planning Task Force will poll the congregation on this Objective and on the naming of a special task force to help the church reach its Objective.

(b) The Planning Task Force will contact various age-level groups to get the names of nine or ten persons to nominate as members for the special task force.

(Name) will contact women's circles, classes, and organizations to secure the names of three persons.

(Name) will contact men's classes and organizations to secure the names of three persons.

(Name) will contact youth organizations to secure the names of two persons.

(Name) will contact one of the junior church school teachers and secure the names of one or two junior children to serve on the special task force.

(c) The Planning Task Force will poll the church on naming persons to the special task force.

(d) The congregation will vote:

(1) Whether it wants this Program Plan at this time.

(2) Whether it approves working with the special age-level task group nominated by the Planning Task Force.

(e) The special task force will elect its own chairperson.

(f) The chairperson will lead the special task force to plan and suggest certain fund-raising events to the church for its approval.

(g) The congregation will approve or reject each event recommended to it.

(h) The special task force will carry out each approved event, making progress reports to the church moderator and the Planning Task Force chairperson, submitting a final report by (date) .

5. *Where will this happen?*

Both church and community will be the setting for the project to raise $1,000.

6. *What will be different?*

Our church members and other interested community members will have responded to a challenge to relieve hunger.

(Example)

Category F: Making our church life more productive and efficient through improved operations.

1. *Objective: Short Term*—Within six months decide how to cut costs in heating our building.

Program Plan: The Board of Trustees will study our building heating plant and the way we use our building to recommend ways to cut costs. These recommendations will be given to the congregation for review and approval.

2. *Who will make this happen?*
   (a) The Board of Trustees.[3]
   (b) The congregation.

3. *When will this happen?*

   The Board of Trustees' study will be completed by   (date)   . An interim report of progress will be available by   (date)   . The congregational vote will be on or before   (date)   .

4. *How will this happen?*

   The Board of Trustees will design the pattern it will use to study our current procedures and will decide whether a consultant's help is needed. If so, an estimate of consultant costs will be secured.

   Field trips to churches which have already cut their costs may be made. All proposals for new procedures will be presented to a congregational business meeting.

5. *Where will this happen?*

   The initial study will be limited to our heating plant and building use; however, if certain churches have effected dramatic savings, the Board of Trustees may take a field trip to observe firsthand what they have done.

6. *What will be different?*

   It will cost less to maintain our building without sacrificing comfort.

REVIEWING PROGRAM PLAN DETAILS

STEP 3:3

Each Program Plan Manager should present a copy of the completed Program Plan Details to the Planning Task Force for its review. The Planning Task Force is responsible to see that each proposed set of Program Plan Details is complete and fits the intention of the Objective and the Program Plan. The Program Plan Details worksheet should then be returned to the Program Plan Manager after the Planning Task Force has approved it.

---

[3] The chairperson serves as Program Plan Manager.

(Sample Worksheet)

PROGRAM PLAN DETAILS

Category: _____

1. Objective: _____

     Program Plan: _____

     _____

     _____

2. *Who* will be involved in making this happen?

     _____

3. *When* will this happen? (Start?   Finish?)

     _____

4. *Where* will this happen?

     _____

5. *How* will this happen? (What will persons *do* to make this happen?)

     _____

     _____

     _____

6. *What* specifically *will be different or changed* if "what happens" is successful? (Relate to your criteria.)

     _____

     _____

Date written: _____ By whom: _____

Approved by: _____ Date: _____

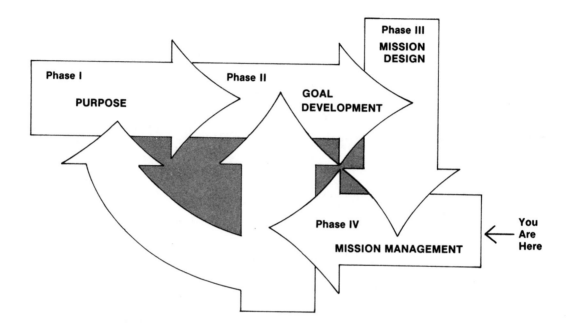

Phase IV
Mission Management

STEP
4:0

INTRODUCTION

A vision, however arrived at, demands realization in some concrete form. If the vision or its realization is faulty, we call the result bad art—or bad management; if the realization [matches] a good vision, we call it a masterpiece—or effective management. The point is an obvious one: the source of good management is found in the imagination of leaders, persons who form new visions and manifest them with a high degree of craft. The blending of vision and craft communicates the purpose. In the arts, people who do that well are masters. In business they are [managers.]

. . . To manage is to lead, and to lead others requires that one enlist the emotions of others to share a vision as their own. If *that* is not an art, then nothing is.[1]

Successful planners are the ones who "plan their work and work their plans." In Phase I through Phase III you have built your plan. Your *plan* is now your tool for action. Your plan, however, is not a machine which will run itself. As Boettinger implies above, translating your vision (your Program Plan) into action requires managers. Managers are people who get things done. Managers are people who keep their vision in mind while giving attention to details. Program Plan Details require close attention if they are to be used to move people toward their chosen objective.

Mission Management has two levels:
1. Management of each Objective and its Program Plan.
2. Management of the entire set of Program Plans.

Program Plan Managers are needed to handle the first level, each managing a Program Plan and its details. A Program Coordinator is needed to handle the second level, coordinating the work of all Program Plan Managers.

PROGRAM PLAN MANAGER

Each Program Plan should have its own manager. Each Program Plan Manager, working with others, is responsible *to design* and carry out his or her Program Plan Details, *to monitor* what is happening, *to make* progress reports to the Program Coordinator, and *to submit* a final evaluation report through the Program Coordinator to the Planning Task Force.

PROGRAM PLAN MANAGERS SHOULD:
1. Understand and be committed to the planning process you are using.
2. Be committed to the Objective and its Program Plan.
3. Develop the Program Plan Details and submit them to the Planning Task Force for approval.
4. Carry out the Program Plan Details, as approved.

---

[1] Henry M. Boettinger, "Is Management Really an Art?" *Harvard Business Review,* January/February, 1975.

5. Use the details in the plan to check progress in terms of people who should be involved, deadlines that should be met, actions that should be taken, and counts that should be recorded to see if intended changes are taking place.[2]
6. Submit periodic reports to the Program Coordinator. If problems occur, contact the Program Coordinator immediately.
7. Make recommendations to the Program Coordinator whenever the Program Plan Details should be revised because conditions have changed.
8. At all times be able to distinguish between what *is* taking place as compared with what was *intended* to take place.
9. Prepare an evaluation report for the Program Coordinator to use with the Planning Task Force and the congregation when the Program Plan is completed.

WHO CAN BE A PROGRAM PLAN MANAGER?

The Program Plan Manager could be:
1. A member of the Planning Task Force.
2. A member of a board, committee, council, or other group you think should be responsible for a Program Plan.
3. Someone from your congregation suited to manage a particular Program Plan.

STEP
4:2

PROGRAM COORDINATOR

Name a Program Coordinator to whom your Program Plan Managers can relate. Program Plan Managers need someone to whom they can give progress reports with some confidence that the big picture of your church's total ministry will not become blurred by all the necessary detail work.

THE PROGRAM COORDINATOR SHOULD:

1. Understand and be committed to the planning process you are using.
2. Provide orientation for each new Program Plan Manager about how his or her Program Plan is related to all the other Program Plans.
3. Receive reports from and provide guidance to Program Plan Managers.
4. Make periodic reports to the Planning Task Force on progress of all Program Plans under way.
5. Through the church newsletter or other media share with the congregation the progress and/or changes for your church's total program.
6. Review with the Planning Task Force every six months all of the Program Plans being managed to determine whether all categories for your Areas of Concern (see pages 45-46) are covered by what your church is currently doing.
7. Assist the Planning Task Force to keep on target with its priority objectives awaiting the appointment of a Program Plan Manager.
8. Help each Program Plan Manager present the final evaluation report to the Planning Task Force.

WHO CAN BE THE PROGRAM COORDINATOR?

The Program Coordinator could be:
1. The chairperson of your Planning Task Force, a logical choice if that person is willing to serve.

---

[2] For numbers 5 and 9 use the Evaluation Worksheet and the Record of Results Worksheet described in Phase V, pages 86 and 88.

Name a program coordinator to whom your program plan managers can relate.

2. Your pastor, even though his or her work is already time-consuming and comprehensive. (This is a particularly good choice if the congregation, in fact, gives high priority to planning.)
3. A person in your congregation whose skills and experiences make him or her suited for this kind of work. (Add this person to the Planning Task Force.)

SUMMARY

Mission Management is both the Program Coordinator's job and the Program Plan Manager's job. Mission Management turns plans into results. Persons who manage your planning operation are the leaders, who, with patience and gentle firmness, can help your church translate its vision (goals and objectives) into action with successful outcomes.

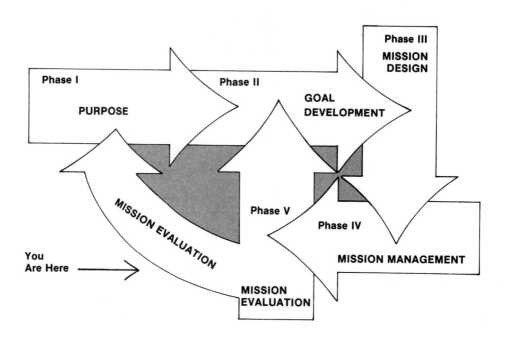

Phase V
Mission Evaluation

STEP
5:0

INTRODUCTION

Evaluation means *considering carefully the worth or "value" of what you have done.* Evaluating programs makes it possible to answer:
- What happened?
- Was it what we wanted?
- Did enough happen to make our work worthwhile?
- What did we do best?
- What would it have been better to do differently?

The Program Plan Manager, with assistance from the Program Coordinator, is responsible for evaluation. These two must cooperate for evaluation to be successful.

The Program Plan Manager will know best what the Program Plan Details require and how the related criteria fit the Objective. In addition, the Program Plan Manager will be involved in preparing progress reports used to assess how well the Program Plan is moving along. Finally, the Program Plan Manager (or someone he or she assigns) will observe, collect notes, hand out and receive questionnaires, and do whatever else is needed to gather and interpret the facts necessary for evaluation.

The Program Coordinator is responsible for receiving progress reports and for working with each Program Plan Manager in preparing the final evaluation report. All evaluation reports should be forwarded by the Program Coordinator to the Planning Task Force.

Program evaluation has five steps:

Step 5:1 reviews pre-evaluation activities you completed in Phases II, III, IV.

Step 5:2 describes *structure, process,* and *product* as a way to organize your evaluation work.

Step 5:3 provides guidance for preparing facts to use in evaluation.

Step 5:4 describes ways to report conclusions from your facts and ways to make recommendations based on them.

Step 5:5 suggests how to build the Big Picture.

STEP
5:1

PRE-EVALUATION ACTIVITIES

This *Manual* calls for certain pre-evaluation activities in earlier Phases. These are beginning points for Mission Evaluation and are reviewed below.

In *Phase II* Step 2:9 , you worked on your objective statements using the ideas that an objective: (1) is a target, (2) is derived from a goal statement, and (3) is worded so movement toward it can be measured.

On pages 58-59 you were asked to get your Objectives ready for use in evaluation by writing criteria for each one. You were asked to consider what exactly was expected or intended by each Objective. You also were asked to decide what should be looked for, observed, counted, or measured in some way as clues or signs (criteria) of: (1) what had been achieved, and (2) how well the Program Plan helped to achieve these ends.

In Step 2:10 you set priorities among your Objectives. Priority guideline #10 (page 61) asked you to consider how clearly each Objective pointed to the clues or signs which should be looked for as evidence of achievement.

In *Phase III* Step 3:2 , you were given the parts needed for a successful Program Plan. Program Plan Managers were instructed to describe *who* were to be involved, *when, where,* and *how;* also *what* would be different or changed if the Program Plan Details were carried out successfully. These descriptions were to be written on worksheets like the one on page 77 for review and approval by the Planning Task Force.

In *Phase IV* Step 4:1 , Program Plan Managers were given the following pre-evaluation responsibilities (as part of a total list of responsibilities):

5. Use the details in the plan to check progress in terms of people who should be involved, deadlines that should be met, actions that should be taken, and counts that should be recorded to see if intended changes are taking place.

8. At all times be able to distinguish between what *is* taking place as compared with what was *intended* to take place.

9. Prepare an evaluation report for the Program Coordinator that can be used with the Planning Task Force and the congregation when the Program Plan is completed.

In Step 4:2 Program Coordinators were asked (among other things) to:

3. Receive reports from and provide guidance to Program Plan Managers.

4. Make periodic reports to the Planning Task Force on the progress of all Program Plans under way.

8. Help the Program Plan Manager present the final evaluation report to the Planning Task Force.

If you carried out these suggestions, you now have material useful for evaluating your Program Plan and its details. Step 5:2 presents a way to organize this evaluation material.

ORGANIZE YOUR EVALUATION WORK

STEP 5:2

In this planning process, you need to evaluate three elements:

ELEMENT 1: How well did you organize to get the job done? This element is called *"structure evaluation."* It deals with the arrangements you make in order to be able to carry out your Program Plan Details. Jesus pointed to this element when He observed that no person plans to build without first sitting down to figure out what it will cost (Luke 14:28, TEV).

ELEMENT 2: How well did things go? We call this element *"process evaluation."* It deals with the actions you took in carrying out your Program Plan Details. It deals with the kinds of things to which Proverbs 4:26 (TEV) refers, "Plan carefully what you do, . . ."

We might well ask: "What happened to people" because of the planning process?"

ELEMENT 3: What changed? We call this element *"product evaluation."* It deals with what comes about as the result of having carried out your Program Plan Details. The New Testament makes several references to this element: "you will know them by their fruits" (Matthew 7:16). "The fruit of the Spirit is love, joy, peace, patience, kindness, goodness, faithfulness, gentleness, self-control" (Galatians 5:22-23). ". . . if it bears fruit . . . well and good; but if not, you can cut it down" (Luke 13:9).

Use these three elements—*structure, process,* and *product*—to organize your evaluation work. This will build a string of evidence between the intention stated in your Objective and the results you achieved from carrying out your Program Plan. The logic of such organization goes something like this:

1. If the *structure* evaluation shows you made the proper arrangements to carry out your process; and
2. If the *process* evaluation shows the steps you planned to take were, in fact, taken and in their proper order;
3. Then there is good reason to assume that what happened, the *product,* was related to what you did.

STRUCTURE EVALUATION

The evaluation of *structure* asks the question "How well did we organize to get the job done?" Your Program Plan Details show what arrangements you *intended* to set up to carry out your program, i.e., the structure you planned to use. For example, if your program was to help persons learn to bake a cake, the structure questions would deal with the kitchen, the stove, the cooking utensils, the recipe books, etc.

Structure evaluation is asking: "How well did we use our buildings, equipment and resource persons to get the job done?"

Examine your Program Plan Details and your filled-in Evaluation Worksheet (page 86). Check your Evaluation Worksheet against the *who, when,* and *where* described in your Program Plan Details:

Were the right people in the right place at the right time with the proper tools and materials so they could take the steps described in the Program Plan Details?

PROCESS EVALUATION

Process evaluation is the next step after the evaluation of structure. Go back to the example of helping someone learn how to bake a cake. The process questions would be, "Did the people *know which* recipe to follow?"

EVALUATION WORKSHEET

Goal: _____

1. Objective: _____

   Program Plan: _____

List specifics as described in your Program Plan Details	What really took place?	If you had to make adjustments from what was planned, what were they? Why were they necessary?
2. Who will be involved?		
3. When will this happen?		
4. Where will this happen?		
5. How will this happen?		
6. What will be different if this happens?	(Use RECORD OF RESULTS Worksheet.)	

"Did they *know how* to follow the recipe?" *"Did* they follow the recipe?" Evaluating the process described in your Program Plan Details changes these questions only a little.

Check your Evaluation Worksheet against the *how* described in your Program Plan Details. Ask such questions as:

- How well did the persons involved know the blueprint of the Program Plan Details?
- Were steps in the Program Plan Details set in proper order, so persons could follow them?
- Did each step take place at the right time?
- Did anyone get mixed up? (Try to find out *why* whenever this type of thing happens.)

PRODUCT EVALUATION

Product evaluation is the final step after you have evaluated structure and process. Again, consider the example of teaching someone to bake a cake. The product questions would be: "Did the cake look appetizing?" "Did it taste good?"

Begin your product evaluation with what you have written on the Record of Results Worksheet, mentioned first on page 80 and shown on page 88. The left side will be filled in with what you have written under Question #6 on your Program Plan Details Worksheet. The right side should be filled in by the time you complete Phase IV, Mission Management. What is written becomes your record of (1) what you *planned to achieve* through the program and (2) what was *actually achieved* through your Mission Management.

RECORD OF RESULTS WORKSHEET
(Completes item #6 of Evaluation Worksheet)

WHAT WE INTENDED TO HAPPEN		WHAT DID HAPPEN	
What change do we want? (outcome or result)	What clues or signs will be used to show this change? (criteria)	What clues or signs did we see?	How much of each sign did we see?

Evaluate the product of your Program Plan by comparing (or contrasting) what is written on the right-hand side of your Record of Results with what is written on the left. If the two sides are alike, you have probably reached your Objective. If they are not alike, you will be able to see how far you fell below, or went beyond, your Objective.

PREPARING FACTS FOR EVALUATION

STEP 5:3

This step has three parts:
1. Defining the facts you need for evaluation;
2. Putting those facts into order;
3. Finding out what this arrangement of facts means.

DEFINING THE NEEDED FACTS

There are two ways to find out things about people. First, you can look at them (observe or measure). Second, you can ask them questions (interview, survey, test). Your design for collecting evaluation facts will be one or the other of these two ways, or some combination of both.

Evaluation is deciding how well you accomplished what was intended when you wrote your objective.

There are three kinds of evaluation facts:

1. Facts about understandings

    —An understanding is something a person has learned, what the person knows and is able to use.

2. Facts about attitudes

    —An attitude is how a person feels about something. It is usually shown through a gesture, a facial expression, a spoken opinion, a tone of voice.

3. Facts about actions

    —Actions are the ways people go about doing things. Sometimes an action shows a new skill or an increase in an already existing skill. It may show a habit is increasing or decreasing. It may show a change in custom, method, or practice.

There are four levels at which facts can be gathered:

1. "Nominal" facts

    These are facts that name. They indicate only whether a thing is present or absent. An example is the numbers on football players' uniforms. The numbers identify the players so that the fans can tell whether a particular individual is on the bench or on the playing field. Nominal facts are numbers that "name."

2. "Ordinal" facts

    These facts let you put things into ranks: first, second, third, and so on.

    To put things into ranks simply means to set in order on some basis of "bigger than"—"smaller than," without having to say exactly what "bigger" or "smaller" may mean.

    A typical example is an elementary school teacher's process of lining up the class for a group photograph. Though the teacher doesn't use a yardstick or a tape measure, he or she has no difficulty putting the tall people in the back row and the short people in the front row.

    Ordinal facts allow persons to make real distinctions without having to be precise about the degree of the distinction.

3. "Interval" facts

    These facts allow you not only to put things into ranks, but you can also describe equal differences between ranks. Interval facts, however, have no way to define what zero means, and no good idea of infinity.

    An example of this is the thermometer a mother uses to take her baby's temperature. The thermometer has no zero point (it would be meaningless for the baby to have a temperature of zero). The thermometer has no infinitely hot point (the baby is not in the middle of the sun). But within these limits the mother knows that each mark on the thermometer is the same distance from the next mark, and she can use the thermometer to tell whether the baby's temperature is normal or whether the baby is running a fever. We find interval facts used in measures of human knowledge or understanding and in tests of mental abilities.

4. "Ratio" facts

    These facts are the kind bankers use.

    Bankers' numbers have a true zero point: you can be in debt to the bank (be below the zero point); you can have a bank account (have money deposited against which you can write checks); you can have no money in the bank (be right at the zero point).

    Bankers' numbers have equal intervals; ten dollars is twice as much as five dollars and one-half as much as twenty.

Bankers' numbers also suggest some working idea of infinity, such as "all the money ever made between creation and the end of the world."

Most church Program Plan evaluations will involve nominal and ordinal facts. Some Program Plans, those involving the work of trustees or persons in stewardship projects, will use ratio level facts. Some church education programs may use interval-type facts.

When gathering facts and figures about understandings, attitudes, and actions, be sensitive to the level at which you are collecting these facts. This will help both those who have the responsibility to observe (or ask questions) and those who are responsible to interpret what the observers record.

Be careful that from the start you know how you are going to use the facts you collect. Do not gather merely interesting facts and figures. A good way to make sure you are collecting *useful* facts is to tie what is being collected to a specific sign or clue used as part of the criteria related to the Objective for the Program Plan.

PUTTING YOUR FACTS INTO ORDER

After you have collected your facts and figures, you may be facing several piles of paper on which the facts and figures have been recorded. These piles must be reduced to some pattern that has meaning. Mainly, this means putting the facts and figures about the same event onto the same sheet of paper (or stapling pages together if several sheets are involved).

If you asked questions for which persons composed their own answers (open-end questions), all answers to the same question should be brought together on one sheet of paper. Then, mark which open-end answers are positive, which are negative, and which are neutral. Next to each recorded answer put some facts that identify the type of person giving the answer (such as age, sex, church leadership responsibility, occupation, grade in school, etc.). These identifying facts will allow you to recognize similarities and differences among the several types of people usually involved in each Program Plan.

You may ask questions to which persons respond by checking one or more answers that you provide (closed-end questions). These answers are easier to reduce into a usable form. Record these answers on a tally sheet listing each type of person answering (man/woman; youth/adult; regular attender/infrequent attender; and so on).

When open-end answers are put into categories, such as "Strongly Agree," "Agree," "Neutral," "Disagree," "Strongly Disagree," the answers can be coded in the same way as closed-end answers. Sort all coded answers into separate piles according to the types of people or their answers; if needed, combine them into other piles, and count each pile.

Several tools can be used for this work. The simplest is an 8½" x 11" sheet of paper on which you draw 80 boxes about ¾ inch square, arranged in eight columns and ten rows, and numbered 1 through 80 across the rows. Reproduce a set of these sheets and use one 80-box sheet for each person answering. Each of the small boxes on a sheet can be used to carry a number that shows the answer to a given question (up to 80 questions). Set up a piling system so that each pile of paper represents a different answer to the same question. For example, the sheets of paper could first be separated between those marked "Male" and those marked "Female." Then each of these two piles could be further sorted between those marking "Yes" and those marking "No" as the answer to a given question. The result of these two "sorts," when counted, would be: (1) the number of "Males" saying "Yes," (2) those saying "No"; (3) the number of "Females" saying "Yes," and (4) those saying "No." Such two-way sorts show any differences in the way in which persons of different sexes answer questions.

Sorting can be done faster by purchasing 3 x 5 inch or 5 x 7 inch cards that come with holes drilled around all four edges. Such cards can be punched to remove the outside edge of the holes, using whatever coding arrangement you wish. A long needle like a knitting needle can then be inserted through a deck of these cards and lifted. Cards which have not been punched to show a certain answer will remain on the needle. Cards which have been punched to show the answer will remain on the table, permitting them to be counted quickly and sorted further, if desired.

Computers are becoming increasingly available to churches. Any of the standard computer-readable materials may be available for your use, such as the 80-column computer card, punched paper tape, magnetic tape cartridges, etc.

The important thing is that your facts, once you have put them into order, should be "captured" in some way to make it possible to separate or to combine and to count the facts you have collected.

FINDING WHAT THESE FACTS MEAN

Now you need to find out what you found out. What things are alike? What things are different? What does it all mean?

This *Manual* identifies four ways to look at your facts, depending on the level at which they were collected (nominal, ordinal, interval, ratio). The first three ways are generally no more complicated than proving your monthly bank statement. The fourth is more complicated. Most church Program Plan evaluations will use only the first two ways. Some Program Plan evaluations need the third and fourth also.

We call the four *counting, figuring, computing,* and *calculating.* The first two are fairly easy. The third is not much more difficult than following the special recipe for your favorite cake. The fourth requires skills of someone trained in mathematics. But there are more and more of these people around, and some of them are active Christians. They would gladly volunteer their skills if local churches gave them an opportunity to do so.

In addition, many low-cost, hand-held calculators have special keys to do automatic calculation of such things as square roots. The time in church program evaluation is at hand for using mathematics to find out what your facts mean. Many elementary schools introduce students to hand-held calculators. Most high schools assume the use of calculators as a basic tool for math and science courses. Your able young people may be willing to help you find out what your evaluation facts mean. *Counting*—the easiest way to find meaning in your facts.

Counting is a skill all of us use. Many persons in their work use a tally system to take inventories. They use four vertical marks with a diagonal line to indicate 5 (as, ‡‡‡‡). The count of these fives multiplied by five gives the total or sum. This simple device is a powerful observation tool for marking the increase or decrease of a sign or clue.

Another type of counting involves the "median"—the middle number in a list that has been put into a ranked order (see page 90). Fifty percent of the numbers will be above the median, and 50 percent will be below.

A third kind of counting deals with the "mode," the category which has the greatest number of tallies of all categories being examined. For example, if "Strongly Agree" has twelve tallies and all other categories have fewer, then "Strongly Agree" is the mode.

Using tallies, sums, medians, and modes requires nothing more than paper and pencil. The only mathematics used is addition. (Counting tally sets by fives, i.e., 5-10–

15-20-etc., is easier for some persons than multiplying; do it either way—you will get the same answer.)

Figuring—not quite as easy as counting, but almost.

Figuring includes:
- graphs
- charts
- percents
- the average (the "mean," the sum of all scores divided by the number of scores being added)
- ratios (a way of relating one thing to another using simple fractions)

Most junior high school math books give instructions on how to use these figuring tools. A handy book for adults who have been out of school for a while is *Mathematics for Practical Use, A Simplified Guide,* by Kaj L. Nielsen. It is available in paperback (Barnes and Noble, Inc., Everyday Handbooks No. 212).

Computing—a little more difficult than figuring; get one of your able high school students to help.

Computing involves arranging facts into patterns (known as "arrays") by scores, ranks, or categories. Once facts are in an array, you can compute the difference between averages, the relationship between two groups, and the likelihood that a trend may exist.

For your use (or that of the high school student) we suggest two helpful pamphlets issued by the Union College Character Research Project.

These pamphlets give simple recipes for finding out what your facts mean. They were designed for use by lay persons in local churches. One pamphlet is *Basic Tools for Creative Research, Designed for the Layman to Use in Solving Everyday Problems in an Objective Way.* The second pamphlet is *Data Analysis, Statistical and Technical Aids.* Each pamphlet can be purchased for less than $2.50 by writing to: Character Research Project, 207 State St., Schenectady, NY 12305.

Calculating—Is there an engineer in your congregation? An insurance actuary? A high school math teacher? A sociologist? Someone who just likes mathematics?

Calculating involves advanced mathematical skills. It includes variance analysis, factor analysis, multiple regression analysis, etc. Many churches have members whose occupations require them to work with mathematics at the calculating level. If you know of such persons, this part of your evaluation work can allow them to use their talents for the church in a new way.

Each Program Plan Manager should put his or her evaluation facts together. Use the *kinds of facts, levels of facts,* and *ways to arrange them* which best fit the Program Plan Details. When this work is completed, the Program Plan Manager is ready for Step 5:4 .

REPORTING CONCLUSIONS AND RECOMMENDATIONS

STEP 5:4

Evaluation involves reporting conclusions and recommendations based on facts and figures you have collected, reduced, and studied. It is the way church planners make decisions about future Program Plans.

You are now ready to draw conclusions, using what you have learned from your evaluation facts.

- Did we make the right arrangements? (structure)
- Did we take the right steps? (process)
- Did we achieve the intended result? (product)

Your evaluation report should include the answers to these three questions. In this way you are accounting for your stewardship of resources used in the Program Plan.

Your evaluation report should also include your recommendation concerning the future of the Program Plan. Your recommendation may be one of four types:

- Repeat, because . . .
- Revise, because . . .
- Replace, because . . .
- Stop, because . . .

Complete the appropriate sentence for the type of recommendation you make. Submit your evaluation report to the Program Coordinator for use by the Planning Task Force at its next meeting.

THE BIG PICTURE

STEP
5:5

Over a period of time the Planning Task Force will receive several Program Plan evaluation reports whose Objectives come from the same goal. When looked at together, these reports from Program Plan Managers will begin to build a big picture showing movement toward one Goal.

In addition, your church probably has several Program Plans under way, which are related to different Goals. At least once a year the Planning Task Force should look at all Goals for which Program Plan evaluation reports have been received. By examining recommendations related to Objectives for all of the Goals, the Planning Task Force can begin building a bigger picture of how well the church's life expresses what is said in its Purpose Statement.

As we compare what our church is doing with what our purpose statement says, we will be in a position to re-examine the statement itself.

When you have worked through several evaluations in this planning cycle, you will probably want to review your Goals and Objectives. From time to time you may even want to rephrase your Purpose Statement. Moving through a series of planning cycles does not mean just doing the same tasks over again but planning on the basis of new information, new insights, and new skills gained by following this *Manual.*

A Second Cycle of Planning

A local church Planning Task Force should periodically recycle certain planning Steps . It should return to Step 2:6 and review assumptions at least every three years. All later steps in the planning process would then be followed, based on any changes made in the assumptions.

At least every six years the Planning Task Force should return to Step 2:3 and update the data gathered about the church, the community, and the world. In light of these new data, a new Information Summary can be prepared and later planning steps taken. Needless to say, the second time around will likely be less time-consuming.

As you become familiar with this planning process, it will be easier to use. Through planning, may God guide you to a challenging future in which your church is more effective by

- Stating your purpose
- Writing your Goals and Objectives
- Developing your Program Plans (and details)
- Managing your mission
- Evaluating your progress.

The planning process needs to be a continuing part of church life.

LOCAL CHURCH PLANNING MANUAL
List of Appendixes

ADDITIONAL READING RESOURCES

Anderson, James D., *To Come Alive.* New York: Harper & Row, Publishers, 1973.

The thesis of this book is that congregations must have a structure which allows the greatest amount of productivity.

Anderson, Philip A., *Church Meetings That Matter.* Philadelphia: United Church Press, 1965.

Helps readers understand what turns church and board meetings into good meetings.

Babbie, Earl R., *Survey Research Methods.* Belmont: Wadsworth Publishing Company, 1973.

A basic primer for anyone wanting to engage in survey research; it covers everything from creating a sample to interpreting the results.

Blazier, Kenneth D., and Huber, Evelyn M., *Planning Christian Education in Your Church.* Valley Forge: Judson Press, 1974.

This booklet offers a logical planning process specifically for Christian education programming in the local church.

Conlan, Douglas R., and Varey, J. Douglas, *Planning for More Effective Ministry.* Toronto: United Church of Canada (Department of Planning Assistance).

A simple, yet effective, local church planning manual.

Gallup, George, Jr., and Davies, John O., III, *What My People Think: Gallup Survey Manual.* Princeton: American Institute of Public Opinion, 1971.

This manual, designed for use in local churches, guides the reader through each step of public opinion polling and includes a sample questionnaire.

Mead, Loren B., *New Hope for Congregations.* New York: The Seabury Press, Inc., 1972.

Stresses the role of consultants in problem solving for local churches.

Schaller, Lyle E., *Parish Planning.* New York: Abingdon Press, 1971.

This book offers handles for decision making and beginning the planning process in a local church.

Hey, That's Our Church! New York: Abingdon Press, 1975.

Suggestions as well as descriptions are provided in some interesting case studies about churches which have lost their goals in a changing world.

WILL YOU NEED ASSISTANCE
IN THIS PLANNING PROCESS?

Complete each of the following statements so it best fits your preference or probable action. Don't think long about your choice since your first and immediate reaction is probably more accurate.

Place the letter corresponding to your choice in the "My Choice" blank at the end of each statement. You will be shown how to score your choices when you have finished. Statements marked with an * are for ministers only.

There are no "right" or "wrong" choices. The purpose is to discover the degree of help needed in your use of this planning process. Honesty in completing these statements is essential.

	My Choice	**Score**
1. All other circumstances being equal, I would rather: (a) grow as much of our family's food as possible; (b) purchase as much as possible from the store.	_____	_____
2. If I were able, I would prefer to be: (a) a TV emcee, (b) a TV producer-director.	_____	_____
3. If skills, time, and money made no difference, I would prefer to: (a) build my own house; (b) buy the house already built.	_____	_____
4. If I were a teacher, I would prefer to teach: (a) physical education, (b) geometry.	_____	_____
5. I am the kind of person who prefers to: (a) do a job myself; (b) teach someone else how to do it; (c) ask for volunteers and let them do the job on their own.	_____	_____
6. I usually get up each morning: (a) before 7 A.M.; (b) between 7 and 8 A.M.; (c) after 8 A.M.	_____	_____
*7. If I were not a minister, I would most likely have a job where: (a) I could set my own schedule and assignments: (b) I could work on an hourly basis and be told what to do; (c) I could be paid a salary and work as a supervisor or department head.	_____	_____
*8. I am strongest in: (a) preaching, (b) visitation, (c) administration.	_____	_____
*9. In relationship to our Sunday church school I feel: (a) I know the people, leaders, materials, and what is happening; (b) I am removed and not familiar with what is happening; (c) I am involved in planning, training, or teaching.	_____	_____

		My Choice	Score

10. If time and money were not important and I had and used a fireplace, I would rather: (a) cut and haul my own wood; (b) purchase the wood and have it delivered to my home.   _____   _____

11. My leisure reading is usually: (a) books under 200 pages in length; (b) books over 200 pages in length; (c) newspapers and magazines.   _____   _____

12. If I purchased a bicycle, I would prefer that: (a) it come already assembled; (b) it come disassembled so I could put it together.   _____   _____

13. When sitting in meetings where I am not in charge or have little or no responsibility, my tolerance level is usually reached after: (a) 1 hour, (b) 2 hours, (c) 3 hours or more.   _____   _____

*14. I usually plan my sermon topics: (a) week by week, (b) one or two months at a time, (c) three months or more at a time.   _____   _____

15. The person who manages my finances is: (a) myself, (b) another, (c) another and myself jointly.   _____   _____

16. If asked what my personal and/or professional goals are for the next 1–5 years: (a) I could say definitely; (b) I could not say; (c) I would have a general idea.   _____   _____

17. When operating a new machine or appliance for the first time, I usually: (a) read, reread, and carefully follow the operator's manual; (b) figure I know how to operate it and proceed to do so, reading the manual only if I have problems.   _____   _____

18. Given a fairly normal week, those closest to me: (a) know at all times where I can be reached in case of an emergency; (b) do not know where to reach me.   _____   _____

*19. In planning a worship service, I would prefer (a) to choose a theme and then fit hymns, sermon, Scripture, etc., around it; (b) to write the sermon and then fit the rest of the service around it; (c) to use a published guide for worship services.   _____   _____

20. I would rather be: (a) a newspaper sports reporter, (b) a newspaper photographer, (c) a newspaper editor, (d) a newspaper publisher-manager.   _____   _____

21. If age, talent, and money were no problem, I would rather be: (a) a professional baseball player, (b) a professional baseball manager, (c) a professional baseball club owner-general manager.   _____   _____

	My Choice	Score

22. In games, what counts most to me is: (*a*) playing to win, (*b*) being with people, (*c*) having fun.

23. If I were given $50,000, I would most likely: (*a*) spend most on some things I've wanted for a long time; (*b*) spend some but deposit most in a bank; (*c*) invest all of it.

*24. I use the following amount of time most weeks in preparing for the Sunday morning sermon: (*a*) under 2 hours, (*b*) 2-3 hours, (*c*) 3-4 hours, (*d*) 4 or more hours.

25. I: (*a*) enjoy putting together difficult picture puzzles; (*b*) do not enjoy this activity.

*26. I prefer: (*a*) to keep my work schedule flexible and not be tied to a pattern; (*b*) to set a definite schedule and stick to it except for emergencies.

27. If able, I would rather be: (*a*) a physical education teacher, (*b*) a librarian, (*c*) a high school principal, (*d*) a superintendent of schools.

28. I believe a car owner should: (*a*) try to do most of his/her own service and repairs; (*b*) have someone else work on the car.

29. In solving a problem, I prefer to: (*a*) work with the smallest group possible; (*b*) work on the problem alone; (*c*) involve the maximum number of persons.

30. What I know about systematic planning: (*a*) turns me on; (*b*) turns me off; (*c*) gives me mixed feelings.

31. When people ask questions in meetings: (*a*) I am annoyed; (*b*) I feel good; (*c*) I am not affected.

32. I would prefer to: (*a*) put together a TV kit; (*b*) buy a TV from a store.

33. My vacations are usually planned by: (*a*) myself, (*b*) another, (*c*) myself and others.

34. If given a choice, I would rather: (*a*) watch TV; (*b*) read a good book; (*c*) do something with another person.

35. If the washing machine breaks down, I would: (*a*) attempt to fix it myself; (*b*) call a technician without trying to fix it myself; (*c*) tell someone else to fix it or to call a technician; (*d*) forget about it for a while and suggest the laundry be done at the laundromat.

	My Choice	Score

36. Regarding this questionnaire: (*a*) I think I know what it is trying to determine; (*b*) I'm not really sure; (*c*) I really don't know and don't particularly care.   _____   _____

SCORING

Note: Listed below is the number of each statement and possible choices. Each choice has a point value. Using this list as a guide, put the point value of your choice to each statement in the blank provided. Then add the total points and place that figure in the blank opposite the words "Total Score."

You will then be informed about what your total score means.

Statement Choice	Point Value	Statement Choice	Point Value	Statement Choice	Point Value
1 a	2	*14 a	1	25 a	2
b	1	b	2	b	1
2 a	1	c	3	*26 a	1
b	2	15 a	2	b	2
3 a	2	b	1	27 a	2
b	1	c	3	b	1
4 a	1	16 a	3	c	3
b	2	b	1	d	4
5 a	1	c	2	28 a	2
b	3	17 a	2	b	1
c	2	b	1	29 a	2
6 a	3	18 a	2	b	1
b	2	b	1	c	3
c	1	*19 a	3	30 a	3
*7 a	1	b	2	b	1
b	2	c	1	c	2
c	3	20 a	1	31 a	1
*8 a	2	b	2	b	3
b	1	c	3	c	2
c	3	d	4	32 a	2
*9 a	2	21 a	1	b	1
b	1	b	2	33 a	2
c	3	c	3	b	1
10 a	2	22 a	2	c	3
b	1	b	3	34 a	1
11 a	2	c	1	b	2
b	3	23 a	1	c	3
c	1	b	2	35 a	4
12 a	1	c	3	b	3
b	2	*24 a	1	c	2
13 a	1	b	2	d	1
b	2	c	3	36 a	3
c	3	d	4	b	2
				c	1

If you are not a minister, disregard scoring those numbers with an *

Total Score _____

SCORE INTERPRETATION SHEET

Maximum Score—for ministers   100
                —for non-ministers   89

Minimum Score—for ministers   36
                —for non-ministers   29

If your score was between 75–100 and you are a minister
                      or
               65–89 and you are a non-minister:
You will most likely be able to use this planning process with a minimum amount of difficulty.

If your score was between 60–74 and you are a minister
                      or
               50–64 and you are a non-minister:
You will most likely need the help of a consultant at strategic points as you use this planning process.

If your score was between 36–59 and you are a minister
                      or
               29–49 and you are a non-minister:
You will most likely need the help of a consultant throughout your use of this planning process.

SOME EXAMPLES OF PURPOSE STATEMENTS

The six purpose statements included in this Appendix represent different approaches to purpose writing. Some are long; some are short. Some include traces of "programming"—something we do not recommend. Purpose statements should fulfill both of the following principles:

1. Emphasize the "vertical" relationship.

2. Avoid references to particular methods of ministry.

The statements are presented only as examples. Including them in this Appendix does not mean we suggest you consider using them as your own. Write your own purpose statement: live with it, study it, refine it, and make it yours!

Example 1 (observes both principles)

In response to God's call, it is the purpose of the _____ Church with those who share a commitment to Jesus Christ as Savior and Lord to be a community through which the Word of God (logos) may be revealed.

Example 2 (observes both principles)

God calls us to continue Christ's ministry as a community of Christian love. We shall respond.

Example 3 (ignores principle 1)

We are working together as a congregation to be a church of Jesus Christ—a church which diligently and without arbitrary distinctions seeks and welcomes into membership any who love and follow the Lord, a church which enlists leaders and workers according to human talents, a church which embodies Christlike concern for all people it can reach in the Master's name, beginning with those who live within its neighborhood.

Example 4 (ignores principle 2)

We are a church which belongs to Jesus Christ, and he is our Lord and Savior. He calls us to faith in God our Father, and life in the Holy Spirit. He commands us to love one another as he loves us. He calls us to be faithful in worship and in teaching his truth. He calls us to minister to the world in his name and to witness to his saving power in the midst of human life. In all ways, we shall praise Jesus Christ.

Example 5 (ignores principle 2)

In obedience to God's call to participate in his reconciling work through Jesus Christ, the members of this congregation undertake corporately to:

1. Be a caring community of persons seeking to live under the lordship of Jesus Christ;

2. Act responsibly with other churches and secular agencies to meet human need and to alleviate social ills;

3. Express the Good News of Jesus Christ so that persons are called to commit their lives to him;

4. Facilitate the world mission of our denomination as a responsible member of the family;

5. Challenge each member toward more faithful expression of the gospel.

Example 6 (ignores both principles)

The purpose of this church shall be the advancement of the kingdom of Jesus Christ. It shall seek to attain this end through the public worship of God, the preaching of the gospel, consistent Christian living by its members, personal evangelism, missionary endeavor, and Christian education.

ADDITIONAL SCRIPTURES FOR
STUDY OF PURPOSE

These Scripture passages supplement those included in the main text on page 23. The passages listed below focus on the nature of the church and what it should do.

1. Isaiah 1:1-20
2. Matthew 16
3. Matthew 18:18-20
4. Matthew 26:26-29
5. Matthew 28
6. Mark 11:25, 26
7. Mark 16:16
8. Luke 4:16-19
9. John 2:21
10. John 20:21-22
11. Acts 1:1-14
12. Acts 2:42
13. Acts 12:5, 12

14. Acts 14:27
15. 1 Corinthians 13
16. Ephesians 1:21, 2:22, 5:25
17. Colossians 1:2, 18
18. 1 Thessalonians 2:12
19. 1 Timothy 6:17-19
20. Titus 1:9-13
21. Titus 2:14
22. Titus 3:1, 8, 14
23. Hebrews 9:12
24. James 1:17-27
25. 1 Peter 1:1-25
26. 1 Peter 2:4-10

CHURCH PROGRAM REVIEW

Your church offers many programs to its members. Your Planning Task Force should find out the following:

- What programs do we offer?

- How do these programs relate to each other?

- How do those who plan and carry out these programs feel about them?

- What do our boards and committees want to recommend to the Planning Task Force?

The attached forms will help you gather this information. Give them to boards, committees, or individuals who can help you look at your programs. Get as many leaders involved in this process as you can. The program categories are:

1. Evangelism

2. Finance and Stewardship

3. Christian Education

   a) Children's Ministries

   b) Youth Ministries

   c) Adult Ministries

4. Worship and Devotional Life

5. Music

6. Missions

7. Cooperation with Other Churches

8. Participation in the Life of the Community

9. Property Management (land, buildings, equipment)

Church Program Review

1. EVANGELISM

1. Who is responsible for planning the evangelism program in your church?

   _____

2. How many persons were baptized by your church during each of the past five years?

   /_____ /_____ /_____ /_____ /_____
   Year No.   Year No.   Year No.   Year No.   Year No.

3. Do you feel your church wants to grow numerically? ☐ Yes ☐ No

4. How does your church discover prospective new members? _____

   _____

5. Who is responsible to record the names and addresses of persons who visit your

   church? _____ What kind of follow-up is made on visitors?

   _____

6. What have been the main sources of new members over the past five years? (such as church school, visitation evangelism, etc.)

   _____   _____

   _____   _____

   _____   _____

7. What proportion of the persons who joined your church during the past two years were related to persons who were already church members? (such as children of members, etc.)

   _____%

8. If you see a pattern in your answers to questions 6 and 7, does the pattern suggest a need for new styles of evangelism or simply more of what you are now doing?

   ☐ New styles   ☐ More of what we are doing

9. Does your church use evangelism resources produced by your denomination? ☐ Yes ☐ No.

   If "yes," what contribution have these resources made to your church?

   _____

10. What are your congregation's strengths in evangelism? List.

_____   _____

_____   _____

_____   _____

11. How well does your evangelism program make use of these strengths? (For instance, if you have members with skills in visitation, do you provide opportunities for them to use such skills?)

_____

_____

12. How does your church help its members discover their evangelistic strengths, develop new skills, and use them? _____

_____

_____

13. What are your congregation's weaknesses in evangelism? List.

_____   _____

_____   _____

14. Do you feel all church boards and committees have a common responsibility for evangelism? ☐ Yes ☐ No.

In terms of carrying out its responsibility for evangelism, what is the relationship between your board (or committee) and the others in your church?

_____

_____

15. Have you ever discussed with other program units the implications of evangelism for their work? ☐ Yes ☐ No. If not, do you feel you should? ☐ Yes ☐ No. If "yes," when could this begin?

_____ .

NOTE: The Bible talks about *witness* in three arenas:

1. Service (diakonia)—Matthew 20:26
2. Fellowship (koinonia)—Ephesians 4
3. Proclamation (kerygma)—Mark 1:14-15; 16:15
                           1 Corinthians 1:18-25
                           2 Corinthians 4:5
                           2 Timothy 4:1-2

16. List which of these arenas your church is using in its ministry of evangelism.

    _____ _____ _____

17. How is your church *serving* your community? _____

    _____

    _____

18. How is your church providing *fellowship* opportunities for your community?

    _____

    _____

19. How is your church *proclaiming* the gospel to your community?

    _____

    _____

20. What plan do you follow to discover new residents in your community?

    _____

    _____

21. How long has it been since your church participated in a community-wide religious

    census? _____ Is one needed in your community now? ☐ Yes

    ☐ No.

22. What image do you feel your community has about your church?

    _____

    How do you know what this image is? _____

23. Does your community feel that your church *really* cares about it? ☐ Yes ☐ No.
    Does it? ☐ Yes ☐ No. How can you tell?

    _____

24. In reference to fellowship, how do the members of your congregation support or

    minister to one another? _____

    _____

25. What kinds of experiences does your church provide for members:

    —to know each other? _____ _____

    —to trust each other? _____ _____

    —to serve each other? _____ _____

26. Regarding "proclamation," by what means does your church tell the story of what God is doing in the world through Jesus Christ?

    _____

    _____

    _____

27. How often (in the last five years) have you provided training for visitation evangelism? _____ What training methods have you used? _

    _____

28. Do you hold evangelism services or preaching missions annually? ☐ Yes ☐ No.

29. Write below any questions, suggestions, or comments you want to give to the Planning Task Force about your program of evangelism.

(This form, when completed, should be returned to the chairperson of the Planning Task Force: _____.)

Church Program Review

2. FINANCE AND STEWARDSHIP

1. How is the annual church budget prepared? _____

   _____

   By whom? _____

2. By what methods do you secure support for your church budget?

   _____

3. List *each* organization within your church which has its own budget.

   _____   _____

   _____   _____

   _____   _____

4. List the stewardship materials/resources used last year in your church and/or church school.

   _____   _____

   _____   _____

   _____   _____

5. What proportion of your membership uses an offering envelope system?

   _____%

   ☐ Check here if your church does not use an offering envelope system.

6. Has your local church budget grown each of the past three years? ☐ Yes ☐ No. If "yes," by what percent each year? _____% _____% _____%

7. Has your mission budget grown at the same rate? ☐ Yes ☐ No. If "no," by what percent each year? _____% _____% _____%

8. Who in your church determines how much of its income shall be given to the work of local, national, or international mission? _____

   _____

9. Do you receive any income from endowments or commercial property? ☐ Yes
☐ No. How much? $_____ What part of this, if any, was used for your
program last year? $_____

10. Do you use church suppers or sales to raise money? ☐ Yes ☐ No. If "yes," how
much was raised in this manner during the past year? $_____

11. Have you developed a program of "time stewardship" in your church? ☐ Yes
☐ No. If "yes," describe this program. _____

_____

_____

12. Does your church maintain a "skill bank" in which the skills of members are
recorded for church and community leadership roles? ☐ Yes ☐ No. If "yes," how
current is the listing? ☐ Current ☐ Out-of-date.
If current, how well do you feel the church is using the skill bank? ☐ Effectively
☐ Somewhat effectively ☐ Not effectively

13. How does your group work with Christian education leaders to promote
stewardship education? _____

_____

14. Write below any questions, suggestions, or concerns you want to give to the
Planning Task Force about finances and stewardship.

(This form, when completed, should be returned to the chairperson of the Planning
Task Force: _____.)

Church Program Review

3. CHRISTIAN EDUCATION

1. Do you have an appointed or elected unit responsible for Christian education?
   ☐ Yes ☐ No.

2. How is this unit organized? In other words, does it have age level or other subcommittees? Does it use task forces? Consultants? Etc.

   Describe. _____

   _____

   _____

   _____

3. What are the educational goals and objectives for your church's education program?

Goal	Related Objectives
_____	_____
	_____

Goal	Related Objectives
_____	_____
	_____

4. What areas of your church life are the responsibility of your educational unit?

   _____ _____ _____

   _____ _____ _____

   _____ _____ _____

5. What curriculum materials are used in your church school? _____

   _____

   Who selects curriculum materials? _____

6. Our church school is: growing ☐, holding its own ☐, declining ☐.

   If it is not growing, what do you think are the reasons? List.

   _____   _____

   _____   _____

   _____   _____

   _____   _____

7. Is lay leader development a responsibility of your educational unit? ☐ Yes ☐ No.

8. What has been done in the past year to provide growth experiences for your church

   leadership? _____

   _____

   _____

   _____

9. What special events or programs are the responsibility of your educational unit? (Such as camping, conferences, vacation church school, schools of mission, etc.) List each and describe strengths and weaknesses.

   Event or Program _____

   Strengths _____

   Weaknesses _____

   Event or Program _____

   Strengths _____

   Weaknesses _____

   Event or Program _____

   Strengths _____

   Weaknesses _____

10. How does your educational unit rate the following?

	EXCELLENT	GOOD	FAIR	POOR
The overall quality of your church's educational experiences				
The number and variety of educational programs offered				
What you do in children's ministries				
What you do in youth ministries				
What you do in adult ministries				
What you do in leader training				
What you do in family life education				
The community's image of your educational ministries				
The future of your educational ministries				

11. Write below any questions, suggestions, or comments you want to give to the Planning Task Force about your church's Christian education ministries.

(This form, when completed, should be returned to the chairperson of the Planning

Task Force: _____ .)

Church Program Review

3.a CHILDREN'S MINISTRIES

1. How satisfied are the following with your church's educational opportunities and programs for children?

    The children themselves: _____

    Their parents: _____

    The educational unit: _____

    The pastor: _____

2. List the strengths of your ministries with children.

    _____   _____

    _____   _____

    _____   _____

3. List the weaknesses.

    _____   _____

    _____   _____

    _____   _____

4. What percent of the total educational budget is used for ministry with children?

    _____%

5. What percent of your time, effort, and money is expended for and with children *within* your church family? _____% What percent is expended for and with children *outside* your church family? _____%

6. The persons who work with children in your church:

    ☐ are enthusiastic about their work.

    ☐ are discouraged.

    ☐ can't wait to be replaced when their "term" is up.

7. Write below any questions, suggestions, or comments you want to give to the Planning Task Force about your church's ministries with children.

(When completed, this form should be returned to the chairperson of the Planning

Task Force: _____ .)

Church Program Review

3.b-1 YOUTH MINISTRIES *

1. How satisfied are the following persons with your church's program of youth ministries?

   The youth: _____

   Their parents: _____

   The educational unit: _____

   The pastor: _____

2. List the strengths of your ministries with youth.

   _____   _____

   _____   _____

   _____   _____

3. List the weaknesses.

   _____   _____

   _____   _____

   _____   _____

4. What percent of the total educational budget is used for ministry with youth?

   _____%

5. What percent of your time, effort, and money is expended for and with youth *within* your church family? _____% What percent is expended for and with youth *outside* of your church? _____%

6. The persons who work with youth in your church:

   ☐ are enthusiastic about their work.

   ☐ are discouraged.

   ☐ can't wait to be replaced when their "term" is up.

---

*This form should be given to the educational unit responsible for youth ministry.

7. Write below any questions, suggestions, or comments you want to give to the Planning Task Force about your church's ministries with youth.

(When completed, this form should be returned to the chairperson of the Planning

Task Force: _____ .)

Church Program Review

3.b-2 YOUTH MINISTRIES*

1. Which of the words below describes how you feel about your church?
   ☐ Super-great! ☐ Great! ☐ Good ☐ Not-so-good ☐ Awful

2. Which of the words below describes how you think other youth in your church feel about it?
   ☐ Super-great! ☐ Great! ☐ Good ☐ Not-so-good ☐ Awful

3. List the things you like best about your church.

   _____   _____   _____

   _____   _____   _____

4. List the things you do not like about your church.

   _____   _____   _____

   _____   _____   _____

5. Do you feel that youth are generally heard by the leaders of your church? ☐ Yes ☐ No. If not, what do you recommend?

   _____

   _____

6. Are young people willing to assume responsibilities in the life of your church? ☐ Yes ☐ No. If "yes," list some things youth are doing.

   _____   _____

   _____   _____

   If "no," explain why. _____

7. How many young people in your church have a concern for youth who are not in any church? ☐ Most ☐ Some ☐ Few. How is this concern demonstrated?

   _____

   _____

---

*This form should be completed by individual members of your youth groups and/or classes. Reproduce the number of copies you need.

8. Write below any questions, suggestions, or comments you want to give to the Planning Task Force about your church's ministries with youth.

(When completed, this form should be returned to the chairperson of the Planning

Task Force: _____.)

Church Program Review

3.c ADULT MINISTRIES

1. Who coordinates adult ministries in your church? _____

2. How satisfied are the adults of your church with the educational opportunities and programs offered them?

    The young adults: _____

    The middle-aged adults: _____

    The older adults: _____

    The educational unit: _____

    The pastor: _____

3. What method(s) of evaluation is used to determine effectiveness of adult ministries?

    _____

4. List the strengths of your adult ministries.

    _____   _____

    _____   _____

    _____   _____

5. List the weaknesses.

    _____   _____

    _____   _____

    _____   _____

6. List adult classes or organizations which meet regularly for educational purposes at stated times. (e.g., Men's Bible Class, Philathea Class, etc.) State the usual attendance for each.

    Name of class or organization   Attendance

    _____   _____

    _____   _____

    _____   _____

    _____   _____

    _____   _____

7. Small groups emerge from many areas of church life. Some are planned; some are not. List each group by name and give its usual attendance.

Name of Group   *Attendance*

a. *Study and Discussion Groups:* Meet for a series of weeks until study is completed.

     _____ _____

     _____ _____

b. *Family Groups:* Deal with needs of home life, parent-child relationships, etc., e.g., marriage enrichment, family clusters, etc.

     _____ _____

     _____ _____

     _____ _____

c. *Bible Study Groups* (Include those not listed in #6 above.)

     _____ _____

     _____ _____

d. *Prayer Groups:* Meet specifically for silence, meditation, personal and group prayer.

     _____ _____

     _____ _____

e. *Reflection-Action Groups:* Meet together for reflection and planning; then work on action projects and evaluate their experiences.

     _____ _____

     _____ _____

     _____ _____

f. *Koinonia Groups:* Members share life with each other on the "feeling" level; learn to listen and communicate at deep personal levels; and develop an atmosphere of mutual trust and love.

     _____ _____

     _____ _____

     _____ _____

     _____ _____

g. *Fellowship Groups:* Meet to have fun; have a good time getting together.

     _____ _____

     _____ _____

h. *Recreation Groups:* Get together because they bowl, play softball, throw darts, etc.

     _____ _____

     _____ _____

i. *Outreach Groups:* Gather specifically to attract and draw unchurched persons into the life of the church.

     _____ _____

     _____ _____

8. Write below any questions, suggestions, or comments you want to give to the Planning Task Force about your church's ministries with adults.

(When completed, this form should be returned to the chairperson of the Planning

Task Force: _____.)

Church Program Review

4. WORSHIP AND DEVOTIONAL LIFE

1. List: your scheduled worship services
   what, in general, you hope to accomplish in each service
   Rate: each worship service, using "excellent," "good," "fair," or "poor"

Worship Services	*Hope to Accomplish*	*Rating*
_____	_____	_____
_____	_____	_____
_____	_____	_____
_____	_____	_____

2. Describe your worship goals and objectives.

Goal	Related Objectives
_____	_____
	_____

Goal	Related Objectives
_____	_____
	_____

3. How and by whom are your worship goals established? _____

_____

_____

4. Who is responsible for planning your scheduled worship experiences?

_____

5. How do you evaluate whether your worship experiences are meeting the needs of those who attend?

_____

_____

6. List your worship services and average attendance figures for each service over the last three years.

Service	Attendance Last Year	Attendance 2 Years Ago	Attendance 3 Years Ago
_____	_____	_____	_____
_____	_____	_____	_____
_____	_____	_____	_____

Note increases or decreases and give reasons why.

_____

_____

7. What nonscheduled, informal worship experiences are available to your congregation? Describe.

_____

_____

8. In what other settings does your church provide worship experiences? (i.e., homes of those in your congregation who can no longer attend your church services, homes for the elderly, jails, state hospitals, mobile home parks, etc.). List each and indicate who is responsible for it.

Worship Setting	Sponsor/Coordinator
_____	_____
_____	_____
_____	_____
_____	_____
_____	_____

9. In what ways do laity participate in planning or leading your worship experiences?

_____

10. In what ways does your Christian education program support your worship? How do classes or groups teach children, youth, and adults about worship?

_____

_____

11. How does your membership feel about your worship services? Are changes indicated?

   _____

   _____

12. Write below any questions, suggestions, or comments you want to give to the Planning Task Force about the worship and devotional life of your church.

(This form, when completed, should be returned to the chairperson of the Planning

Task Force: _____ .)

Church Program Review

5. MUSIC

1. Does your church have a group appointed or elected to supervise its music program? ☐ Yes ☐ No.
   If you do, what are its functions?

   _____   _____

   _____   _____

2. How do persons become members of this group?

   _____

   _____

3. List your church's choirs. How many persons are in each?

   Name of Choir   *Number of Members*

   _____   _____

   _____   _____

   _____   _____

   _____   _____

   _____   _____

4. Are your choir directors and organists paid? ☐ All ☐ Some ☐ None.

5. Which hymnal do you use in your major worship service? _____

   _____

6. What types of hymns and songs are most often used in your worship services?

   _____

   _____

7. Do you introduce new types of hymns and songs to your congregation from time to time? ☐ Yes ☐ No. If "yes," how?

   _____

   _____

8. Do you use musical instruments other than organ and piano in your worship services? ☐ Yes ☐ No. Do instrumental groups participate in worship services? ☐ Yes ☐ No. In social events? ☐ Yes ☐ No.

   List and describe your congregation's response to each.

   Instrument or Group   *Response*

   _____   _____

   _____   _____

   _____   _____

9. Do you sponsor a church band or orchestra? ☐ Yes ☐ No.

10. Is there potential in your church for a band, an orchestra, or small musical groups? ☐ Yes ☐ No. List.

    _____   _____

    _____   _____

11. Are your organ, piano, etc., of good quality? ☐ Yes ☐ No. In good repair? ☐ Yes ☐ No.

12. Do you sponsor small singing groups (i.e., trios, quartets, etc.)? ☐ Yes ☐ No. Are they ever invited to take part in worship or other experiences? ☐ Yes ☐ No.

13. Do musical groups from your church share in worship or programs in other settings (e.g., another church, nursing homes, association meetings, camps, etc.)? ☐ Yes ☐ No. If "yes," describe when, where, and how often.

    _____

    _____

14. What percentage of your local expense budget is designated for your ministry of

    music?   _____%

15. Write below any questions, suggestions, or comments you want to give to the Planning Task Force about your church's music ministries.

(This form, when completed, should be returned to the chairperson of the Planning

Task Force: _____.)

Church Program Review

6. MISSIONS

1. Define the term "Mission" as you think it is understood by your church.

   _____

2. Do you have an appointed or elected unit responsible for missions? ☐ Yes ☐ No. If "yes," list its responsibilities.

   _____   _____

   _____   _____

   _____   _____

   If "no," who handles mission concerns in your church?

   _____

3. What percentage of your total church budget is given to international, national, and local missions? _____%

   How and by whom is this decision made? _____

   _____

4. Who decides what persons or groups will receive your mission dollars?

   _____

5. What percentage of your mission budget is given directly to your denomination(s)?

   _____%. What percentage of your mission budget is given outside your

   denomination(s)? _____%.

6. What percentage of your mission giving is sent directly to institutions supported by your denomination (e.g., colleges, seminaries, retirement homes, etc.)?

   _____%.

7. Does your church actively encourage support of missions? ☐ Yes ☐ No.

   If "yes," how is this done? _____

   _____

8. Over the past two years, has your "wider mission budget" (national and international missions): ☐ increased, ☐ stayed the same, ☐ decreased? Indicate

   how much increase or decrease $_____.

   List reasons:

   _____ _____ _____

9. Who makes progress reports on mission giving to the congregation?

   _____

   How is this done? _____

   How do you feel about the way it is done? _____

10. How often does your church send its missions money to your denomination? ☐ monthly ☐ quarterly ☐ other.

11. Does your church participate in the One Great Hour of Sharing Offering? ☐ Yes ☐ No.

12. Does your church have an annual missions emphasis (Missions Conference, School of Missions, Missions Emphasis Sunday, etc.)? ☐ Yes ☐ No.

    Describe _____

13. List the methods of mission education used by your church with various age levels.

    _____ _____

    _____ _____

14. Does your church have active "mission circles" or "mission groups"? ☐ Yes ☐ No.

    How many? _____

15. Do the women of your church raise special mission gifts? ☐ Yes ☐ No.

    How much was given in this way in the past two years? $_____.

16. Does your men's fellowship have mission programs to encourage interest in and support for missions? ☐ Yes ☐ No.

    If not, why? _____

17. In what ways are missions emphasized in your youth ministries?

    _____

    _____

18. Does your church encourage attendance at any missions conference sponsored by your denomination? ☐ Yes ☐ No.

   How many persons have gone from your church in the last three years?

   _____

19. Are books on missions in your church library? ☐ Yes ☐ No.
   Do you alert your congregation to these books? ☐ Yes ☐ No.
   How often do you place such new books in the library? ☐ Often ☐ Once in a while ☐ Rarely.

20. Does your church use resource persons for mission emphasis? ☐ Yes ☐ No.

21. Is education in missions of your denomination a normal part of your church school curriculum? ☐ Yes ☐ No.

22. Write below any questions, suggestions, or comments you want to give to the Planning Task Force about your program of missions.

(This form, when completed, should be returned to the chairperson of the Planning

Task Force: _____.)

Church Program Review

7. COOPERATION WITH OTHER CHURCHES

1. Describe each instance during the past year when your church cooperated in some way with a neighboring *church of your own denomination(s).*

   _____   _____

   _____   _____

   _____   _____

2. Describe each instance in the past year when your church cooperated in some way with a *church of another denomination(s).*

   _____   _____

   _____   _____

   _____   _____

3. Cooperative work among churches of your community mainly results from (check one):
   A few interested persons ☐   A few concerned churches ☐
   A ministerial association ☐   A council of churches ☐
                         Other ☐

4. In what way did your church participate this past year in the life of any clustering of churches within your denomination? List the various events or activities.

   _____   _____

   _____   _____

   _____   _____

5. In what ways did your church participate this past year in the life of any other clustering of churches to which it may belong?

   _____   _____

   _____   _____

   _____   _____

6. How many of your members attend the meetings, serve in leadership roles, or become involved in other ways in the life of each clustering of churches?

   Denominational cluster _____   Any other cluster _____

7. How much money did your church give last year to the work of such groups?

   Denominational $_____ Any other $_____

8. In what ways do you feel that the work of your denominational clustering is especially important to the members of your congregation?

   _____   _____

   _____   _____

9. In what ways do you feel that cooperation with churches of other denominations is important to the members of your congregation?

   _____   _____

   _____   _____

10. Write below any questions, suggestions, or comments you want to give to the Planning Task Force about your cooperation with other churches.

(This form, when completed, should be returned to the chairperson of the Planning

Task Force: _____.)

Church Program Review

8. PARTICIPATION IN THE LIFE OF THE COMMUNITY

1. List community agencies which your church officially supports or with which it cooperates (i.e., scouting, 4-H, jails, Salvation Army, Red Cross, Contact, etc.).

   _____   _____   _____

   _____   _____   _____

   _____   _____   _____

2. Are your church members encouraged to express their Christian faith by taking part in community activities? ☐ Yes ☐ No.

   Who encourages them? _____

   How are they encouraged? _____

   _____

3. What do you feel is your church's image in the community?

   _____

   _____

4. Within the past two years, what specific contributions has your church made to solving problems in your community?

   _____   _____

   _____   _____

   _____   _____

5. What goals and objectives does your church have for social action or Christian concern?

Goal	Related Objectives
	_____
	_____

Goal	Related Objectives
_____	_____
	_____

6. Does your congregation ever use community facilities other than its own? ☐ Yes ☐ No.

7. Check below each group outside your church organization which uses your church building for regular meetings, special programs, etc.

____ Scouting

____ 4-H

____ Day Care Center

____ Nursery School

____ Older Adult Groups

____ The Retarded

____ Fraternal Organizations

____ Youth Groups

____ Disaster Relief

____ The Handicapped

Other (please name)

_____

_____

8. For each of your church organizations which has tried to respond to the needs of your community in the past year, list the need, the organization, and what it is doing.

Need _____ Who responded? _____

What is being done? _____

Need _____ Who responded? _____

What is being done? _____

9. Write below any questions, suggestions, or comments you want to give to the Planning Task Force about your participation in the life of your community.

(This form, when completed, should be returned to the chairperson of the Planning

Task Force: _____ .)

Church Program Review

9. PROPERTY MANAGEMENT

1. How does your church use its building space? How often are rooms occupied? Is full use being made of space? Could there be some improvements? For a thorough review, the following table should be completed:

Space/ Room	Program Function	Aver. Attend.	Sq. Ft. of Space	Actual Sq. Ft. per Person	Recommended Sq. Ft. per Person*	Hours of Use per Week	Recommendation(s) Regarding Use of Space

2. Is the site owned by the church adequate? Is there sufficient off-street parking to meet building code requirements and the needs of the church? (Approximately 300 sq. ft. is required for each parking space and the access to it.) Does the church have some open, recreational-type space available? Is there room for expansion? Is there easy, safe access to the building and parking? To review site use, the following table should be completed:

Total Size of Site	Space Occupied by Buildings	Space for Parking	No. of Cars	Other Parking Available	Amount of Open Space	Recommendation(s) Regarding Site

3. Is your church building over 50 years old? ☐ Yes ☐ No. If "yes," has a registered, structural engineer checked its overall condition in the past five years?   ☐ Yes ☐ No.

4. Did the fire inspector note any needed corrections in the last inspection? ☐ Yes ☐ No. If "yes," have corrective measures been taken? ☐ Yes ☐ No.

5. Is the insurance for the church adequate in light of current construction costs?

   ☐ Yes ☐ No. If "no," by how much are you underinsured? $_____.

6. Do you have an Inventory List of all furnishings and equipment for insurance purposes? ☐ Yes ☐ No. If "yes," is this list regularly updated? ☐ Yes ☐ No. Is it kept in a safe location outside the church building (such as a safe deposit box)? ☐ Yes ☐ No.

   Where is it kept? _____

*Contact your denomination's area office if you do not have this information.

Here is an example of a furnishings and equipment inventory form (the numbers circled are items in good condition). Several of these forms could be prepared by the church office for this inventory.

	addressograph	air conditioners	blackboards	bookcases	Bibles	books (study)	bulletin boards	cabinets (file)	cabinets (storage)	chairs (folding)	chairs (children)	chairs (rocking)	chairs (office)	coatracks	choir robes	Communion table	Communion trays	couches	cribs	cupboards	desks	desk racks	drink'g fount'ns
Nursery		1		3	1	60	3		3		19	2							6	4	1		
Kindergarten			2	1	25	6			1	1	27		1							1	1		
Church Office	1	1						2				1	2	1							1	2	
Library				1		450	2	4			6	3		2									
Sanctuary						1					27					1							
Choir Room		1						1	3	35				1	67						2		
etc. . . .																							
TOTALS	1	3	2	5	27	516	5	7	7	69	49	2	1	6	68	1			6	7	3	2	

7. What has been the cost of building maintenance, insurance, and utilities for the past several years? Prepare a five-year record (using the following items) of these costs and determine the trend. This information will be helpful in future budget planning:

Item

Years

	19__	19__	19__	19__	19__
Fuel (gas, oil, coal, etc.)	$_____	$_____	$_____	$_____	$_____
Electricity	_____	_____	_____	_____	_____
Water and Sewage	_____	_____	_____	_____	_____
Insurance Premiums	_____	_____	_____	_____	_____
Pest Control	_____	_____	_____	_____	_____
Cleaning Supplies	_____	_____	_____	_____	_____
Custodial Service	_____	_____	_____	_____	_____
Repairs and Maintenance	_____	_____	_____	_____	_____
Other _____	_____	_____	_____	_____	_____
Totals	$_____	$_____	$_____	$_____	$_____

8. Have those responsible for property management investigated facility improvements that would reduce utilities costs? ☐ Yes ☐ No. (Over the "life cycle" of a building, some minor improvements can result in major savings). Here is a checklist of improvements to consider for both dollar savings and energy conservation. (Check the ones you have done.)

_____ insulation (8″ to 12″ in ceiling, 4″ to 8″ in exterior walls)
_____ storm windows (including over stained glass)
_____ caulking around windows and doors
_____ reduced thermostat settings, especially in unused spaces
_____ yearly cleaning and checking of heating system, pilot light, filters, etc.
_____ zoning the heating/air conditioning system(s)
_____ energy conservation reminders attached to light switches and thermostats
_____ the possibility of solar energy for hot water and/or space heating
_____ subscription to an energy conservation magazine

9. Does the church have any current mortgage indebtedness? ☐ Yes ☐ No. If "yes," what are the facts?

current amount of mortgage (principal) $_____
monthly payments (principal & interest) $_____
interest rate   _____%
mortgage maturity   (pay-off date) _____

10. Write below any questions, suggestions, or comments you want to give to the Planning Task Force about your church's ministry of property management.

(When completed, this form should be returned to the chairperson of the Planning

Task Force: _____.)

TABLES AND GRAPHS
FOR STEP 2:3

(These materials have been adapted from the church and community study packet which was originally developed by the staff of the American Baptist Board of National Ministries.)

INSTRUCTIONS FOR GRAPHS

For Graphs on Pages 157 and 159

To prepare line graphs, find the largest number to be entered in the graph. Divide this number by 15 and then *raise* this result to the nearest 10. E.g., 462 divided by 15 = 31, raise to 40. Each interval on the graph would equal 40.

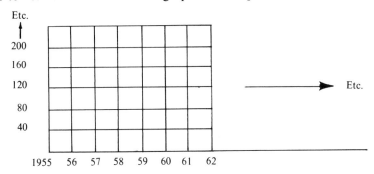

For Graph on Page 171

The financial support line graph can follow the same rule by indicating at the top of the graph that all numbers are multiples of thousands of dollars. The top left-hand corner of the graph looks like this:

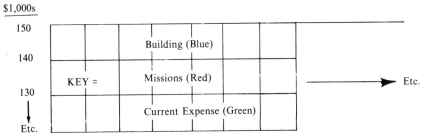

For Graphs on Pages 163 and 211

To prepare double-bar graphs, first compute percentages and then divide the bar among the categories listed on the graph. Each inch represents 12.5%.

	Baptism or Confirmation	Letter	Other
Gain	48.6%	39.0%	12.4%

	Death	Letter	Erasure
Loss	18.9%	45.0%	36.1%

For Graph on Page 167

To prepare the church school profile graph, enter your key for the top half of the graph based on the largest number found in the Nursery to Senior High enrollment. There are 17 spaces in the table, so that most churches are able to use intervals of 4 or less.

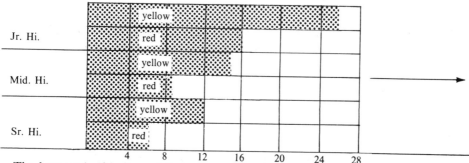

The bottom half is figured the same way but is based on the larger enrollment for either adults or children and youth. Most churches can use intervals of 10 or less.

For Graph on Page 175

To prepare the weekly giving profile, determine first the percentages asked for in the contribution table by family units. Then mark a key at the bottom of the graph for percentage intervals. Most churches can use intervals of 2%.

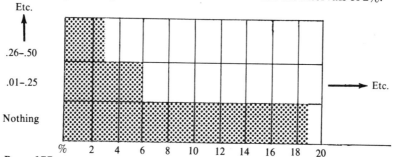

For Graph on Page 177

To prepare the circle graph for distribution of the church dollar, again use percentages.

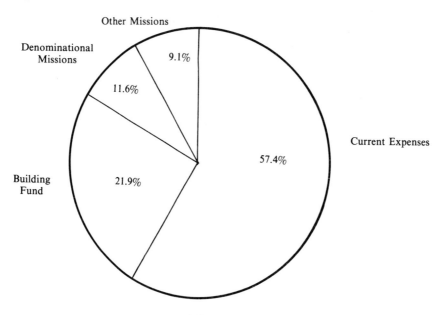

For Graphs on Pages 191, 201, and 203

To prepare age-sex distribution charts, again use percentages. Follow the formula presented on the lower-half of page 189 for working these percentages. Then enter in each chart a line to represent the distance from the center equivalent to the percentage for each age group. For example:

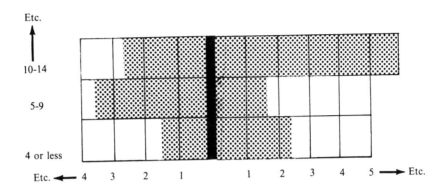

CHURCH AND CHURCH SCHOOL MEMBERSHIP TABLE—TWENTY YEARS

List the church and church school membership for the past twenty years or for the period of time the church has been organized, whichever is greater. The church records should show these figures, but if they do not, check for them in your denominational annual reports. In case your church library does not have copies on hand, the denominational office in your area will have them on file.

If all categories are not available, be sure to obtain those which are a matter of record. For example, not all churches will have average attendance figures for the worship services. Also, not all churches will have lists of active members and of resident members.

Year	Total Members	Active Members	Resident Members	Nonresident Members	*Average Attendance	Church School Enrollment	Average Attendance
19							
19							
19							
19							
19							
19							
19							
19							
19							
19							
19							
19							
19							
19							
19							
19							
19							
19							
19							
19							

* Average attendance should be for the main worship service of the church. For most churches this will be the Sunday morning service. However, if the main service is at some other time, list attendance, if available, and indicate what service was used. If there is more than one service on Sunday morning, indicate the number of services, and record the total for all Sunday morning services.

MEMBERSHIP

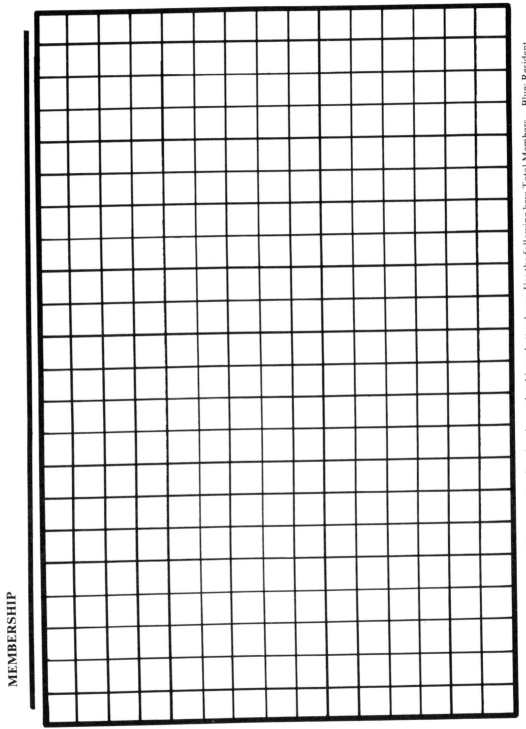

MEMBERSHIP

On the above grid make a line graph showing church membership and attendance. Use the following key: Total Members — Blue; Resident Members—Red; Average Attendance—Green. Arrange numbers from bottom to top along the left margin, and years from left to right along the bottom margin. Start with zero at the bottom and make intervals sufficient to include the largest figure in the table. (See instructions on page 151.)

CHURCH SCHOOL

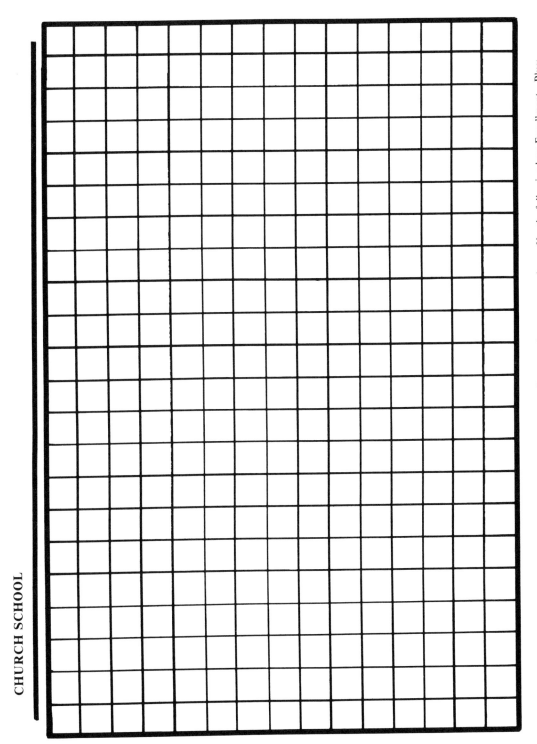

CHURCH SCHOOL

On the above grid make a line graph showing church school enrollment and average attendance. Use the following key: Enrollment—Blue; Average Attendance—Red. Arrange numbers from bottom to top along the left margin, and years from left to right along the bottom margin. Start with zero at the bottom and make enough intervals to include the largest figure in the table. (See instructions on page 151.)

MEMBERSHIP GAIN OR LOSS TABLE—TWENTY YEARS

These figures can be obtained from church records or denominational annuals. Be sure to figure net gain or net loss for each year. Begin with the current year at the top of the page. If fluctuations in figures can be accounted for by factors such as church split, out-migration due to the closing of a mine, factory, etc., attach a note of explanation.

Year	Total Gains	By Baptism or Confirmation	By Letter	By Experience or Other	Total Losses	By Death	By Letter	By Erasure	Net Gain	Net Loss
19										
19										
19										
19										
19										
19										
19										
19										
19										
19										
19										
19										
19										
19										
19										
19										
19										
19										
19										
19										
Totals										
% of Total Gains					% of Tot.Loss				Total Net	

MEMBERSHIP METHODS

MEMBERSHIP METHODS

GAINS

BAPTISM OR CONFIRMATION   – –   LETTER   – –   OTHER

12.5   25   37.5   50   62.5   75   87.5

DEATH   –   LETTER   – –   ERASURE

LOSSES

Make here a double-bar graph, showing membership gains on the top bar and membership losses on the bottom bar. Use percentages, so each bar represents 100%. Divide the bar into segments of different colors to show methods of gain and loss:

    Gains by baptism or confirmation—Red; by letter—Blue; by experience or other—Yellow.
    Losses by death—Red; by Letter—Blue; by erasure or other—Yellow.
    Mark the percentage for each segment. (See instructions on page 151.)

CHURCH SCHOOL PROFILE

Current Enrollment and Average Attendance

(Use Figures for the Last Full Year)

Period Used _____

Department or Class	Grades* or Age	Number Enrolled	Average Attendance
Nursery			
Kindergarten			
Primary			
Middler			
Junior			
Junior High			
Middle High			
Senior High			
Total Children and Youth			
Young Adults			
Adults (list adult classes in order of age group involved)			
Officers and Teachers			
Total Adults			
Grand Total All Departments			

* Indicate here either the grades in public school, or the ages covered by the department or class. NOTE: If a 3-year or a single-year grouping is used, indicate what these groupings are, and fill in the chart ignoring the categories listed at the left, where they do not apply.

CHURCH SCHOOL PROFILE

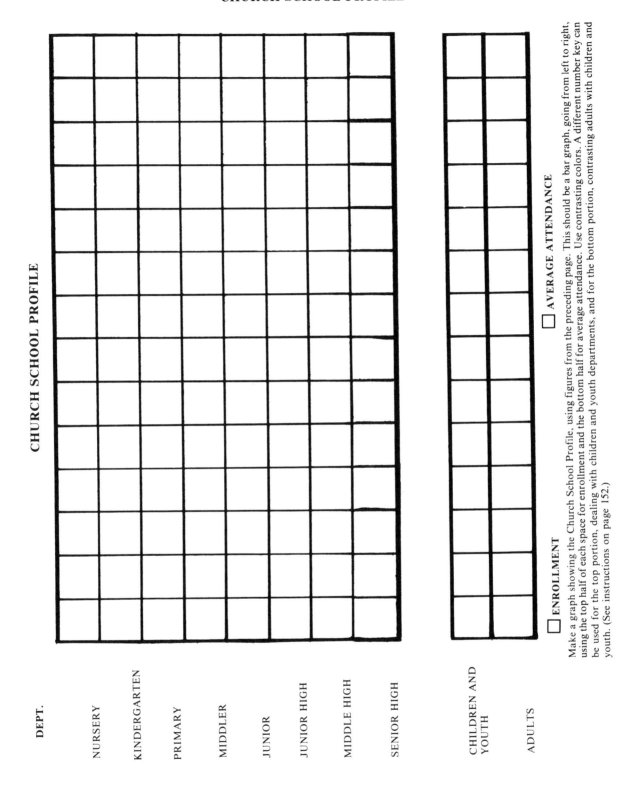

CHURCH SCHOOL PROFILE

DEPT.

NURSERY

KINDERGARTEN

PRIMARY

MIDDLER

JUNIOR

JUNIOR HIGH

MIDDLE HIGH

SENIOR HIGH

CHILDREN AND YOUTH

ADULTS

☐ ENROLLMENT   ☐ AVERAGE ATTENDANCE

Make a graph showing the Church School Profile, using figures from the preceding page. This should be a bar graph, going from left to right, using the top half of each space for enrollment and the bottom half for average attendance. Use contrasting colors. A different number key can be used for the top portion, dealing with children and youth departments, and for the bottom portion, contrasting adults with children and youth. (See instructions on page 152.)

MONEY RECEIVED—TWENTY YEARS

Beginning with the last full year at the top, list under Column A the financial contributions for the past twenty years. This information will be in your annual reports, or it may be secured from annual reports of your denominational office. If money was received from other than members, indicate on a separate sheet how much each year was received from such other sources. Under Column B, figure and enter the amount given for each category for each RESIDENT member. Refer to page 155 for your resident membership figure.

NOTE: These figures are for money received, not for amounts budgeted.

Year	Column A					Column B		
	Total Giving	Local Current Expense	Missions	Building	Resident Membership	Total per Res. Member	*Local Expense per Res. Member	Missions per Res. Member
19								
19								
19								
19								
19								
19								
19								
19								
19								
19								
19								
19								
19								
19								
19								
19								
19								
19								
19								
19								

*Include everything except missions.

FINANCIAL SUPPORT

FINANCIAL SUPPORT

On the above grid make a line graph to show the amounts contributed for various purposes indicated in the key below. Place the lines in order, starting from the bottom, so that the second line will equal the sum of the first line plus the amount of the second item, etc. Thus the top line will represent the total amount of contributions. Label the graph. Arrange dollar amounts from bottom to top along the left margin, and years from left to right along the bottom margin. Current Expenses—Green; Missions—Red; Building Fund—Blue; Other—Black. (See instructions on page 151.)

CONTRIBUTION TABLE BY FAMILY UNITS

In the chart below, indicate the number of "family units" (see Note below) making contributions of record according to the size of the weekly contribution. This information should be available from the Financial Secretary's records. Use the last full year. Year used _____.

If a family unit contributes monthly, or at some other interval, divide the yearly contribution by 52 to determine the amount given weekly. This table should be based on actual dollars received during the last full year, not on the amount pledged for that year.

Amount	Number of Family Units	Percentage of Potential Family Giving Units
		%
$50.01 or more	_____	_____
$30.01 – $50.00	_____	_____
$25.01 – $30.00	_____	_____
$20.01 – $25.00	_____	_____
$15.01 – $20.00	_____	_____
$10.01 – $15.00	_____	_____
$ 7.51 – $10.00	_____	_____
$ 5.01 – $ 7.50	_____	_____
$ 2.51 – $ 5.00	_____	_____
$ 2.01 – $ 2.50	_____	_____
$ 1.51 – $ 2.00	_____	_____
$ 1.01 – $ 1.50	_____	_____
$ .51 – $ 1.00	_____	_____
$ .26 – $ .50	_____	_____
$ .01 – $ .25	_____	_____
Nothing of Record	_____	_____
Total Potential Family Giving Units·	_____	100 %

NOTE: Family units are defined here as one person living alone or several persons living in the same household. However, if a single employed *adult* lives with her/his parents, he/she should be counted as a separate family unit. In families where children of high school age or younger make separate contributions, combine giving of all members of the same family to reach the total for that family unit.

WEEKLY GIVING PROFILE

WEEKLY GIVING PROFILE

Amount																			
$50.01 +																			
30.01 – 50.00																			
25.01 – 30.00																			
20.01 – 25.00																			
15.01 – 20.00																			
10.01 – 15.00																			
7.51 – 10.00																			
5.01 – 7.50																			
2.51 – 5.00																			
2.01 – 2.50																			
1.51 – 2.00																			
1.01 – 1.50																			
.51 – 1.00																			
.26 – .50																			
.01 – .25																			
Nothing																			

On the above form make a bar graph to show the giving profile, using percentages from the previous page. Start with zero at the left, and mark percentages along the bottom margin. (See instructions on page 152.)

DISTRIBUTION OF THE CHURCH DOLLAR

Year _____
(Use last full year)

Indicate how your church divided its income for the last full year.

Local Current Expenses .... $_____   _____%
    Include all local expenses, such as Christian education, etc.

Missions of Your Denomination ....   _____   _____

Other Missions ....   _____   _____
    Attach a list of these other contributions.

Building Fund ....   _____   _____

TOTAL .... $_____   __100__%

Here make a circle graph, beginning at the twelve-o'clock position and moving clockwise, to show the amount of money received for various purposes. Each mark equals 5%. (See instructions on page 152.)

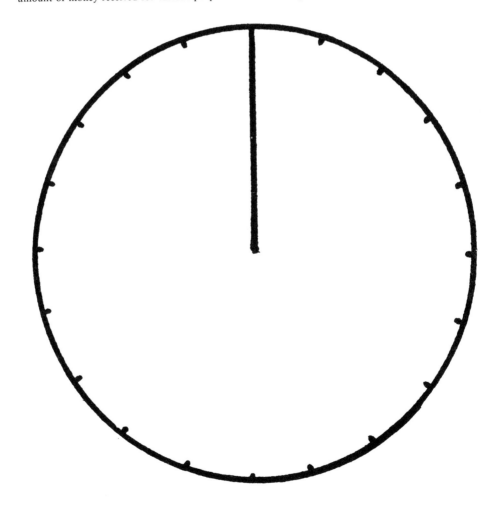

CHURCH PARTICIPATION PROFILE

In order to get a representative picture of your normal worshiping congregation, Church Participation Cards should be used on three successive Sundays in your main worship service. If you have more than one worship service on Sunday morning, they should be used in all services and the results combined. If your main service is at some other time, the cards are to be used then.*

NOTE: Each person is to fill out only one card during the survey. Cards should not be signed. To include all persons in the building during the worship period, use the cards in the nursery, extended session, Junior Church, etc. At least age and sex should be recorded for children in other activities held during your worship hour. Mark these cards to show where the persons were at the time, so that they are not confused with the worshiping group. If it is practical, include other information on the card for such children, though this might be difficult to do. Adults involved in special sessions during the worship hour should fill out a card completely.

In tabulating the cards, the result for those in the worship service should be kept separate from those in other sessions. (For example, there might be nine children from 10 to 14 in the worship service, and thirteen in this age group in the extended session.)

Below are the suggested steps for using the cards:

1. Select three successive Sundays when the congregation will be fairly normal. Avoid Sundays of unusually large attendance, such as Easter, and just before Christmas. Also, try to avoid Sundays of expected low attendance, such as summer or holiday weekends.

2. Distribute cards at a given point in the service** to all worshipers on the first Sunday; to those who have not previously filled out a card on the next two Sundays. *DO NOT* hand out cards with your worship bulletins. Make sure enough pencils are handy. Have people date their cards. Collect cards as soon as they are filled out.

3. The Pastor or a Planning Task Force member should explain the importance of the information to be given and should urge everyone to participate. Have cards filled out while the Pastor or Planning Task Force member stands before the congregation and reads the instructions given on pages 180-181. This will take a little time, perhaps 7 or 8 minutes, but there are no shortcuts to securing this information, and it will be valuable in making your analysis of the congregation.

4. Tabulate the results; record the total for all categories on pages 183, 185, 187, and fill in the table on page 189. To tabulate, proceed as follows:

   a. Divide all cards into age groups found under item 6 on the card.
   b. Either use a blank card or make up a tabulation sheet for *each age group,* and proceed to tabulate cards BY AGE GROUP. When this tabulation is complete, there will be 14 separate sets of results.
   c. Add the totals in each category, and summarize them on the pages provided—pages 183, 185, 187.
   d. Complete page 189, using information under items 4 and 6 on the cards.

NOTE: A count should be made of the number of persons in attendance and the number of cards turned in at each service where the cards are used.

*Cards equal to 1½ times the average attendance will be needed. See page 33 for instructions on how to order cards.

**NOTE: Many churches have expressed concern about the use of these cards in the worship service since it tends to break the continuity of worship. Each church will have to decide for itself the best time to use them. However, there is no substitute for securing this information from the persons who actually attend the worship experience. Using the cards early in the service or at the close may be less of a break in the order of worship. Care should be taken to use the cards when most persons will be present.

SAMPLE CARD

CHURCH PARTICIPATION CARD

Each person fills out only ONE CARD during the participation survey. Complete questions 1-15, others complete questions 1-13.

Complete questions 1-6 for children under the age of 5. Members complete questions 1-13.

Date _____

1. Which one are you?
   _____ Member
   _____ Participating Non-member
   _____ Visitor (_____ first time?)

2. Where did you live when you began to participate?
   _____ Within 1 mile
   _____ 1 to 2 miles
   _____ 2 to 3 miles
   _____ Beyond 3 miles

3. Where do you now live?
   _____ Within 1 mile
   _____ 1 to 2 miles
   _____ 2 to 3 miles
   _____ Beyond 3 miles

4. Sex: _____ Male _____ Female

5. Ethnic Group:
   _____ White _____ Black
   _____ Hispanic _____ Indian
   _____ Asian _____ Other

6. Age: _____ 4 or less _____ 5-9 _____ 10-14
   _____ 15-19 _____ 20-24 _____ 25-29
   _____ 30-34 _____ 35-39 _____ 40-44
   _____ 45-49 _____ 50-54 _____ 55-59
   _____ 60-64 _____ 65 or more

7. Marital status:
   _____ Single _____ Married
   _____ Divorced _____ Widowed
   _____ Separated

8. How long at present address?
   _____ Less than 1 year
   _____ 1 - 2 years
   _____ 2 - 3 years
   _____ 3 - 5 years
   _____ Longer (_____ years)

Rev. 9/76

9. Occupation and Employment:
   _____ Homemaker _____ Student
   _____ Retired _____ Unemployed
   _____ Employed

If now employed, in what category?
   _____ Professional, technical
   _____ Farmer or farm manager
   _____ Manager, proprietor, executive
   _____ Clerical, office, etc.
   _____ Sales worker
   _____ Craft worker, production supervisor
   _____ Operative
   _____ Household worker
   _____ Service worker
   _____ Farm laborer
   _____ Laborer
   _____ Other

10. Your present church responsibilities:
   _____ Church officer or board member
   _____ Church committee
   _____ Church school staff
   _____ Choir member or usher
   _____ Officer of church organization
   _____ Other

11. Church organizations to which you belong:
   _____ Children's _____ Youth
   _____ Women's _____ Men's
   _____ Mixed _____ Other

12. Organizations to which you belong or in which you serve in the community:
   _____ Lodge or auxiliary
   _____ Labor union
   _____ Farm organization
   _____ Professional organization
   _____ Service club
   _____ Scouts, YM, YW, 4-H, etc.
   _____ P.T.A. or school group
   _____ Veterans
   _____ Civic boards, committees, etc.
   _____ Other

13. How many persons now live in your household? _____

14. Your length of membership here:
   _____ Less than 1 year
   _____ 1 to 3 years
   _____ 3 to 5 years
   _____ 5 to 10 years
   _____ Over 10 years

15. Your method of joining this congregation:
   _____ Confirmation
   _____ Baptism
   _____ Letter
   _____ Other

Printed in U.S.A.

180

SCRIPT FOR LEADER WHEN USING CHURCH PARTICIPATION CARD

1. Check if you are a member of this church, a regular participating nonmember, or a visitor. Visitors check also if this is your first time here.
2. Check the distance you lived from the building when you first began to participate. Normally this should be by the most direct route. Estimate if you must.
3. In the same way, check the distance you now live from this building.
   Items 4, 5, and 6 are very important for a successful study. Please complete these questions since cards are not to be signed. Check in front of your appropriate sex, ethnic group, and age category.
   NOTE: Do not continue to answer for children under the age of 5.
7. Please check present marital status:
   Single, if never married.
   Married, if now married.
   Widowed, if husband or wife is dead.
   Divorced, if divorced.
   Separated, if separated.
8. Check how long you have lived where you now live.
9. *Check only one occupation.* If you work at two jobs, check only the one which you consider your main job. If you are a homemaker or a student and are also employed, check which one you consider to be your main occupation. If you are not employed, check whether you are a homemaker, student, retired, or unemployed. If you are employed, check that *and also* the appropriate occupation:
   Professional includes teachers, editors, dentists, clergy, professors, instructors, doctors, lawyers, nurses, architects, librarians, social workers, engineers, etc.
   Farmer or farm manager—self-explanatory.
   Manager (other than farm), proprietor, and executive includes public officials, agents, buyers, officers, floor managers, personnel or credit officers, owners of private business, etc.
   Clerical and office worker—self-explanatory.
   Sales worker includes workers in stores, as well as sales persons on the road.
   Craft worker, production supervisor includes skilled or semi-skilled workers engaged in production, as well as metal workers, etc.
   Operative refers to machine operators in which long apprenticeship is not required, and also truck drivers.
   Household worker refers to those employed in household services.
   Service worker includes firemen, police, barbers, beauticians, janitors, porters, servants, waiters, ushers, soldiers, sailors, coast guard, practical nurses, etc.
   Farm laborer—self-explanatory.
   Laborer includes garage laborers, car washers, stevedores, gardeners, unskilled helpers in construction, manufacturing, etc.
   Other: Check here if you are not sure where you fit, and be sure to indicate your type of work.
10. Check all of your present responsibilities, adapting where necessary to the terminology you use (commission, department, instead of board, for example).
11. These categories are self-explanatory: Note: If Scouts, etc., are sponsored by the church, a check should be placed here by children and youth participating in the church-sponsored unit. If they belong to a unit not sponsored by this church, check under item 12.
12. These organizations in the community are self-explanatory. If an organization to which you belong does not fit any category, list it by actual name.
13. State the number of persons now living in your household unit. (*continued*)

14. Check the category for the number of years you have been a member of this congregation. Estimate, if necessary.
15. Check the method by which you joined this congregation: confirmation, baptism, transfer of letter, or other.

TABULATION SUMMARY SHEET
FOR CHURCH PARTICIPATION CARDS
(3 Sundays)

This is the summary sheet. Combine totals here from age-group tabulation sheets. Record the totals for all groups on this and the following page. Include adults in nursery or extended sessions with the regular participants. Make a special note of children included in special sessions.

	# Cards	
First Sunday	_____	
Second Sunday	_____	
Third Sunday	_____	
Total	_____	
	_____	

1. Which one are you?   #   %
   Member .... _____ _____
   Participating Nonmember .... _____ _____
   Visitor (____first time) .... _____ _____

2. Where did you live when you began
   to participate?
   Within 1 mile .... _____ _____
   1 to 2 miles .... _____ _____
   2 to 3 miles .... _____ _____
   Beyond 3 miles .... _____ _____

3. Where do you now live?
   Within 1 mile .... _____ _____
   1 to 2 miles .... _____ _____
   2 to 3 miles .... _____ _____
   Beyond 3 miles .... _____ _____

4. Sex:
   Male .... _____ _____
   Female .... _____ _____

5. Ethnic Group:
   White .... _____ _____
   Black .... _____ _____
   Hispanic .... _____ _____
   Indian .... _____ _____
   Asian .... _____ _____
   Other .... _____ _____

6. Age:
   4 or less .... _____ _____
   5-9 .... _____ _____
   10-14 .... _____ _____
   15-19 .... _____ _____
   20-24 .... _____ _____
   25-29 .... _____ _____
   30-34 .... _____ _____
   35-39 .... _____ _____
   40-44 .... _____ _____

	#	%
45-49	⎯⎯	⎯⎯
50-54	⎯⎯	⎯⎯
55-59	⎯⎯	⎯⎯
60-64	⎯⎯	⎯⎯
65 or more	⎯⎯	⎯⎯

7. Marital status:

Single	⎯⎯	⎯⎯
Married	⎯⎯	⎯⎯
Divorced	⎯⎯	⎯⎯
Widowed	⎯⎯	⎯⎯
Separated	⎯⎯	⎯⎯

8. How long at present address?

Less than 1 year	⎯⎯	⎯⎯
1-2 years	⎯⎯	⎯⎯
2-3 years	⎯⎯	⎯⎯
3-5 years	⎯⎯	⎯⎯
Longer (⎯⎯ years)	⎯⎯	⎯⎯

9. Occupation and Employment:

Homemaker	⎯⎯	⎯⎯
Student	⎯⎯	⎯⎯
Retired	⎯⎯	⎯⎯
Unemployed	⎯⎯	⎯⎯
Employed	⎯⎯	⎯⎯

If now employed, in what category?	Male	Female	Total	%
Professional, technical	⎯⎯	⎯⎯	⎯⎯	⎯⎯
Farmer or farm manager	⎯⎯	⎯⎯	⎯⎯	⎯⎯
Manager, proprietor, executive	⎯⎯	⎯⎯	⎯⎯	⎯⎯
Clerical, office, etc.	⎯⎯	⎯⎯	⎯⎯	⎯⎯
Sales worker	⎯⎯	⎯⎯	⎯⎯	⎯⎯
Craft worker, production supervisor	⎯⎯	⎯⎯	⎯⎯	⎯⎯
Operative	⎯⎯	⎯⎯	⎯⎯	⎯⎯
Household worker	⎯⎯	⎯⎯	⎯⎯	⎯⎯
Service worker	⎯⎯	⎯⎯	⎯⎯	⎯⎯
Farm laborer	⎯⎯	⎯⎯	⎯⎯	⎯⎯
Laborer	⎯⎯	⎯⎯	⎯⎯	⎯⎯
Other	⎯⎯	⎯⎯	⎯⎯	⎯⎯

10. Your present church responsibilities:

	#	%
Church officer or board member	⎯⎯	⎯⎯
Church committee	⎯⎯	⎯⎯
Church school staff	⎯⎯	⎯⎯
Choir member or usher	⎯⎯	⎯⎯
Officer of church organization	⎯⎯	⎯⎯
Other	⎯⎯	⎯⎯

11. Church organizations to which you belong:

Children's	⎯⎯	⎯⎯
Youth	⎯⎯	⎯⎯
Women's	⎯⎯	⎯⎯
Men's	⎯⎯	⎯⎯
Mixed	⎯⎯	⎯⎯
Other	⎯⎯	⎯⎯

12. Organizations to which you belong   #   %
     or in which you serve in the community:

       Lodge or auxiliary .... ——— ———
       Labor union .... ——— ———
       Farm organization .... ——— ———
       Professional organization .... ——— ———
       Service club .... ——— ———
       Scouts, YM, YW, 4-H, etc. .... ——— ———
       P.T.A. or school group .... ——— ———
       Veterans .... ——— ———
       Civic boards, committees, etc. .... ——— ———
       Other .... ——— ———

13. How many persons now live in your household?

       One .... ——— ———
       Two .... ——— ———
       Three .... ——— ———
       Four .... ——— ———
       Five .... ——— ———
       Six .... ——— ———
       Seven .... ——— ———
       Eight or more .... ——— ———

14. Your length of membership here:

       Less than 1 year .... ——— ———
       1 to 3 years .... ——— ———
       3 to 5 years .... ——— ———
       5 to 10 years .... ——— ———
       Over 10 years .... ——— ———

15. Your method of joining this congregation:

       Confirmation .... ——— ———
       Baptism .... ——— ———
       Letter .... ——— ———
       Other .... ——— ———

NOTE: On the next page fill out the table, using the data from age-group tabulations. Compute percentages by dividing the total number of participants for the three Sundays into the male or female age grouping.

AGE-SEX DISTRIBUTION: Church Participation

Fill in the following table from information on the age-group tabulation sheets for Church Participation Cards, items 4 and 6. Then, make a bar graph to build the distribution pyramid on the following page. Tabulation is described on page 179.

An example of a Table and instructions for working percentages are given at the bottom of the page.

Age Groupings	Total Participants	Male	Female	% Male	% Female
65 and over					
60 - 64					
55 - 59					
50 - 54					
45 - 49					
40 - 44					
35 - 39					
30 - 34					
25 - 29					
20 - 24					
15 - 19					
10 - 14					
5 - 9					
4 or less					
Totals					

Example:

Age Groupings	Total Participants	Male (a)	Female (b)	% Male (c)	% Female (d)
65 and over	243	89	154	8.0	13.8
60 - 64	111	37	74	3.3	6.6
55 - 59	115	42	73	3.8	6.5
50 - 54	106	38	68	3.4	6.1
45 - 49	96	35	61	3.15	5.5
40 - 44	56	13	43	1.2	3.85
35 - 39	40	24	16	2.15	1.4
30 - 34	58	22	36	2.0	3.25
25 - 29	56	28	28	2.5	2.5
20 - 24	69	25	44	2.2	3.95
15 - 19	70	29	41	2.6	3.7
10 - 14	73	23	50	2.1	4.5
5 - 9	12	6	6	0.5	0.5
4 or less	11	5	6	0.45	0.5
Totals	1116	416	700	37.35	62.65

Total—1116. Therefore, divide each number under (a) and (b) by 1116, to arrive at % for columns (c) and (d), thus: 89 (the number of males 65 and over) divided by 1116 equals 8.0%, etc.

It is usually sufficient to carry percentages to only one decimal point. Slight adjustments will sometimes be necessary.

AGE—SEX DISTRIBUTION

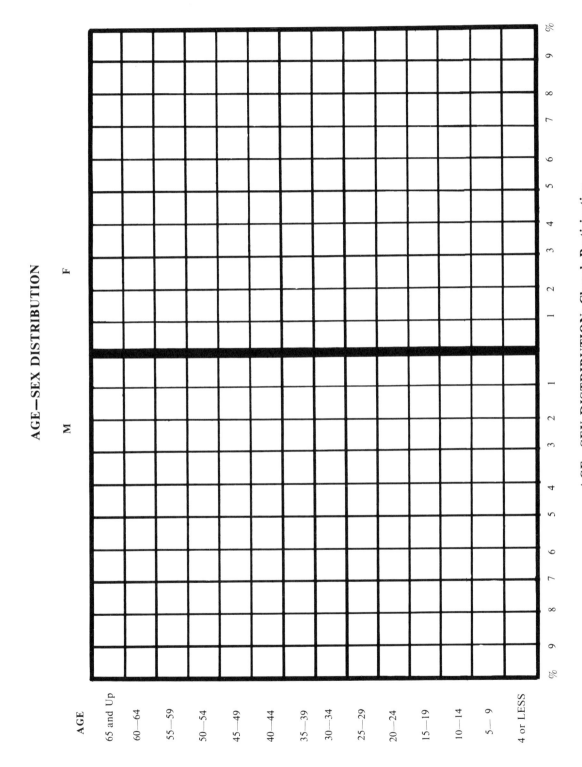

AGE—SEX DISTRIBUTION: Church Participation

Make a bar graph, with the center line as a dividing point, using the information from page 189. (See instructions on page 153.)

CHURCH AREA AND NEIGHBORHOOD: Population Characteristics

The latest census figures can be ordered from the Superintendent of Documents, U.S. Government Printing Office, Washington, DC 20025, or any field office of the Department of Commerce. They are often on file in the reference department of public libraries, or in offices of Planning Commissions, Chambers of Commerce, Social Welfare Agencies, etc. Refer to Appendix G for suggestion of tables to use.

Area: For City churches the *Area* will usually be the city or metropolitan area. For Town and Country situations, the Area may be one or more townships, boroughs, or other civil divisions. By Area is meant the larger community of which the church is a part.

Neighborhood: By *Neighborhood* is meant a smaller geographical area, consisting of not more than one-mile radius around a city church. In a Town and Country situation the Neighborhood will be larger than in a city, but smaller than the Area. In metropolitan areas, the census is reported by small units called Census Tracts. It will take a number of these to make up the neighborhood. Town and Country situations are usually reported by villages, or by townships, etc. Usually the census books include maps to show the divisions used. NOTE: For a city church, include Census Tracts within a one-mile radius of the church. If a tract is split, when more than half is outside the circle, omit it; when more than half is within the circle, include it.

When you need to add Census Tracts or other civil divisions to complete the table below, use the next page to find your totals for the neighborhood.

Area   *Neighborhood*

1. Total Population .... ———— ————
2. White Population .... ———— ————
3. Black Population .... ———— ————
4. Other Nonwhite Population .... ———— ————
*5. Median Income .... ———— *————
*6. Median School Years Completed .... ———— *————

*Record here the median for the high and low tracts or other divisions used.

NEIGHBORHOOD POPULATION TABLE

The following form may be used to find totals for the neighborhood column on the preceding page.

Census Tract or Civil Division	Total Population	White Population	Black Population	Other Nonwhite Population	Median School Years Completed	Median Income
					*	*
Totals						

*Fill in high and low for divisions above.

EMPLOYMENT GROUPS

From the census books, record here the number in each employment group and figure percentages on the basis of the total labor force. NOTE: To arrive at proper totals, it might be necessary to add several tracts or civil divisions together.

	Area*		Neighborhood*	
1. Professional-Technical	Total #_____	_____%	#_____	_____%
2. Managers and Administrators	Total #_____	_____%	#_____	_____%
3. Sales Workers	Total #_____	_____%	#_____	_____%
4. Clerical and Kindred Workers	Total #_____	_____%	#_____	_____%
5. Crafts and Kindred Workers	Total #_____	_____%	#_____	_____%
6. Operatives, except Transport	Total #_____	_____%	#_____	_____%
7. Transport Equipment Operatives	Total #_____	_____%	#_____	_____%
8. Laborers, except Farm	Total #_____	_____%	#_____	_____%
9. Farmers and Farm Managers	Total #_____	_____%	#_____	_____%
10. Farm Laborers	Total #_____	_____%	#_____	_____%
11. Service Workers	Total #_____	_____%	#_____	_____%
12. Private Household Workers	Total #_____	_____%	#_____	_____%
TOTAL LABOR FORCE	Total #_____	_____%	#_____	_____%
Total Females in Labor Force	#_____	_____%	#_____	_____%

*For definition of area and neighborhood, see page 193.

AGE-SEX DISTRIBUTION, AREA AND NEIGHBORHOOD POPULATION

Complete the tables below from the information in the census books. It might be necessary to add several tracts or civil divisions to get totals for each age group. Compute percentages, using the examples provided for Age-Sex Distribution of the Church Participants, found on page 189. Make bar graphs of these two tables on pages 201 and 203.

City or Area*

Age Groupings	Total Population	Male	Female	% Male	% Female
65 and over					
60 - 64					
55 - 59					
50 - 54					
45 - 49					
40 - 44					
35 - 39					
30 - 34					
25 - 29					
20 - 24					
15 - 19					
10 - 14					
5 - 9					
4 or less					
Totals					

Neighborhood*

Age Groupings	Total Population	Male	Female	% Male	% Female
65 and over					
60 - 64					
55 - 59					
50 - 54					
45 - 49					
40 - 44					
35 - 39					
30 - 34					
25 - 29					
20 - 24					
15 - 19					
10 - 14					
5 - 9					
4 or less					
Totals					

*For definition of area and neighborhood, see page 193.

AGE—SEX DISTRIBUTION

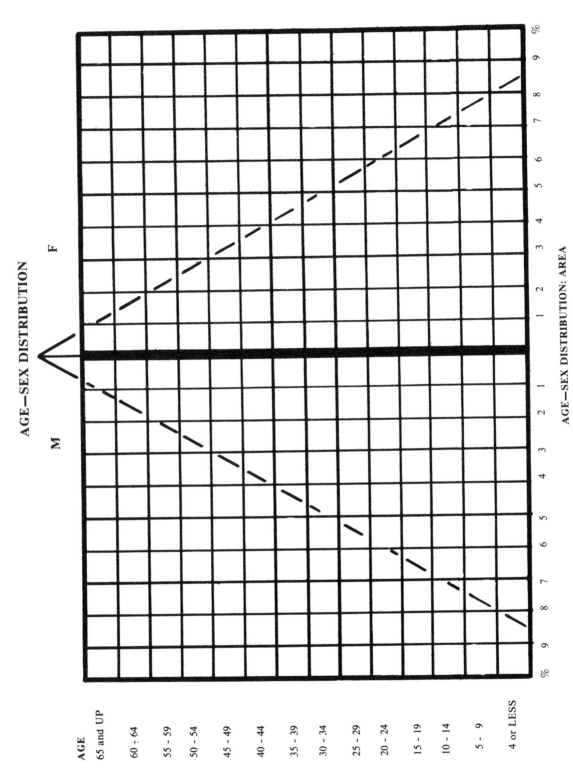

Make a bar graph, with the center line as a dividing point, using information from page 199. (See instructions on page 153.)

AGE—SEX DISTRIBUTION

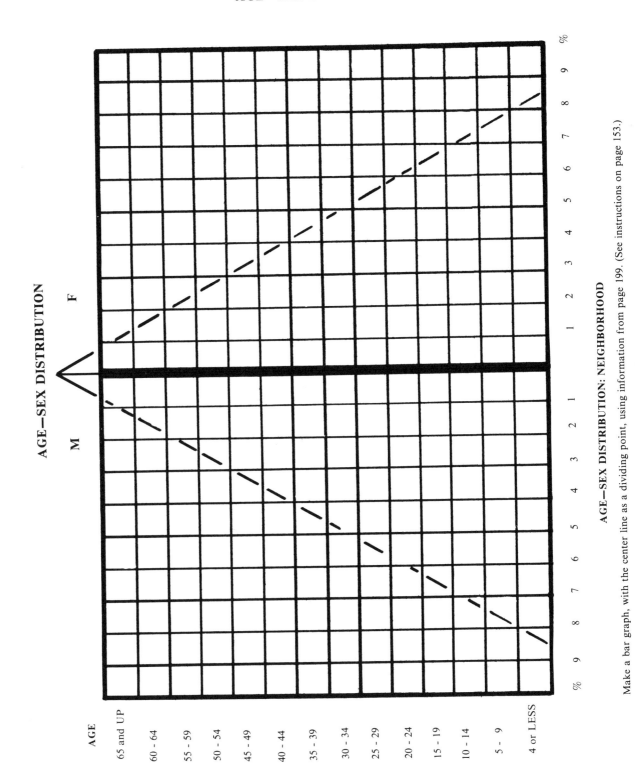

AGE—SEX DISTRIBUTION: NEIGHBORHOOD

Make a bar graph, with the center line as a dividing point, using information from page 199. (See instructions on page 153.)

HOUSING CHURCH NEIGHBORHOOD AND AREA

HOUSING IN CHURCH NEIGHBORHOOD AND AREA

HOUSING: The census reports list statistics on the housing of your city, or area and neighborhood.* In the chart below fill in the data on housing.

	1 Census Tract Number	2 Total Units	3 Owner Occupied	4 Renter Occupied	5 Lacking Plumbing Facilities	6 Median Persons Per Unit	7 Median Value	8 1 Dwelling Unit	9 2 Dwelling Units	10 3 & 4 Dwell. Units	11 5 to 49 Dwell. Units	12 50 or more Dwelling Units	13 1960—Later	14 1950—1959	15 1949—Earlier	16 Median Rent
Neighborhood Total							*	*								*
Area Total																

*Do Not Fill In.

*For definition of area and neighborhood, see page 193.

MAPS

Three maps will be helpful in your planning. Maps without colors are preferred. You can secure maps from your county office or city hall.

NOTE: If maps are expensive or hard to obtain, you might put all your information on a single map. (This approach is not recommended since the result is hard to read.) A map with a scale of 800 feet to the inch is good for a city or metropolitan area. A smaller city might use a larger scale, and a large city might have to use a smaller scale. For a Town and Country situation, a map with a scale not smaller than two inches to a mile should prove satisfactory.

While you prepare maps 1 and 2, also organize your information to complete the tables on page 209.

1. Family or Household Membership Map

   This map should be a clear map, preferably in black and white.
   a. Locate the church building, and draw circles with 1-mile, 2-mile, and 3-mile radii, using the church building as the center.
   b. Locate all households related to the church, using the following key:
      Active household—blue dot.
      Inactive household—red dot.
      Regular participants but not members—green dot.
         (This will include children in church school, or persons in other programs, where no family member is a church member.)

   To make your map more transportable, use colored pencils or felt-tip pens rather than map pins for making dots.

   Definition of a Household or Family: For this map include any family or household where at least one member is related to the church. In some cases two households or families will be housed in the same dwelling unit. In this case, two dots should be used. A widowed person or a single adult should be considered a separate household.

   An Active Family is one in which at least half the family members who are also church members are active. *An Inactive Family* is one in which less than half the family members who are also church members are active. That is, if a husband and wife and teenage son are members of the church, and the husband never attends but the wife and son do, the family should be considered active. There is no universal definition for an active member. Perhaps this planning effort will stimulate the church to make such a definition.

   Especially in Town and Country areas the map scale might be large enough to permit using a dot for each person in the household. Thus a given location might have blue dots for active members, red dots for inactive members, and green dots for those family members who are not church members but who participate.

   As dots are put on, make a circle around each one representing a household in which there is a major church leader—deacon, deaconess, trustee, other board member, officer, choir director, etc.

2. Evangelism Map

   This map should also be a clear map, preferably in black and white. Mark the church location as before, and make circles with one-, two-, and three-mile radii from the church building.

   Locate on this map the residence of all persons who have joined your church during the recent past. Five years should be used, if possible, but the past three years will be sufficient if this is more practical. Designate new members as follows:

   Blue: For persons in households already related to the church through membership.
   Red: For young people whose families are not related to the church through membership.
   Green: For adults with no previous household or family relationship to the church through membership.

   Use one dot for each person.

3. Church Location and Community Factors Map

   This map should also be a clear map, preferably in black and white.
   On this map locate churches of all faiths, including Jewish, Buddhist, etc.
   In a city of more than 10,000 population, locate churches within two miles of the church building.
   In a town and country area, locate all churches in the area covered by the map.
   In any case, locate all churches of your

denomination in the area covered by the map. Use a square and a numbered key (☐) to designate churches.

Also show the following factors:

Blue: Rivers and water areas, including swamps.

Red: Traffic arteries, bus routes, etc.

Green: Parks, golf courses, cemeteries, or other large open spaces, such as the lawn of an institution.

Brown: Business areas.

Yellow: Industrial areas.

Black: Railroads.

WHERE MEMBERS AND CONSTITUENTS LIVE

On page 207 the location of members and nonmember participants was requested. Failure to complete this form at the time the map is being made will result in added work and likelihood of error.

The definition of a household and a way to determine active and inactive families were suggested under map No. 1 on page 207.

Note especially that Section A below will include all households related to the church, even though in some cases a household will contain only one person. Likewise, Section B will include all persons related to the church. In other words, the total result of the table will be to discover, within each geographic distance, the total number of persons related to the church, and the number of households these persons represent.

Distance from Church Building	Section A			Section B		
	ALL MEMBER HOUSEHOLDS			ALL MEMBER PERSONS		
	Active	Inactive	Nonmembers Participating	Active	Inactive	Nonmembers Participating
Within 1 mile						
1 to 2 miles						
2 to 3 miles						
Farther						
Totals						

WHERE NEW MEMBERS LIVED WHEN THEY JOINED

On page 207 an "Evangelism" map was requested. While this is being done, complete the following table. Specify the years being used: 19___ through 19___.

Distance from Church Building	Persons in Already Related Households	Young People in Households Not Otherwise Related	Adults Not Previously Related	Total
Within 1 mile				
1 to 2 miles				
2 to 3 miles				
Farther				
Totals				

DISTANCE FROM BUILDING

DISTANCE FROM BUILDING

WITHIN 1 MILE — 1-2 MILES — 2-3 MILES — BEYOND 3 MILES —

MEMBERS

PARTICIPANTS

12.5   25   37.5   50   62.5   75   87.5

Make a double-bar graph. Show Members (information is found in Section B on page 209) on the top bar, and Worship Participants (information is found in #3 on page 183) on the bottom bar. Use percentages, so each bar represents 100%. Divide the bar into segments of different colors to show distance as follows; then label the graph:

Within 1 mile—Green; 1 to 2 miles—Red; 2 to 3 miles—Yellow; Beyond 3 miles—Blue.

Mark the percentage for each segment. (See instructions on page 151.)

CHURCH HISTORY
Use this form to record historical facts about your church.

Date of Beginning _____ Number of Charter Members _____

Place of First Service _____

How Was Church Begun? Denominational action _____

Regional action _____

Another church _____ Which one? _____

Split from another church _____ Which one? _____

Spontaneous development _____

Colporteur _____ Who? _____

Union of churches _____ Which ones? _____

Other means _____ Explain: _____

Number of pastors serving since beginning (attach list with dates if possible) _____

Names of persons entering Christian service (and dates) _____

_____

_____

When various buildings were erected, or major remodeling was done _____

_____

_____

New churches sponsored by your church _____

_____

_____

Has the church building ever been relocated? If so, indicate various locations, and

when moves were made. _____

_____

Have there been any rifts or splits? _____ When? _____
Describe on a separate sheet.

Were other churches formed as a result? _____

_____

HOW TO GET AND USE U.S. CENSUS REPORTS

You will need various U.S. Census reports to complete the tables and graphs on pages 193 through 205 of Appendix F. Several sources for securing these reports are suggested on page 193 in Appendix F. If you have tried these sources but are unable to gain access to the reports, write for help to: Office of Planning Resources, Board of National Ministries, ABC/U.S.A., Valley Forge, PA 19481. That office maintains a file of all reports from the 1970 U.S. Census, plus many projections and analyses produced by the Census Bureau since 1970.

Another source for census figures is CAPC (Census Access for Planning in the Church). This organization maintains a computerized file of census materials. It is able to provide reports for groupings of census tracts in a metropolitan area or for zip code areas anywhere in the United States. Tables of information can be supplied for the area you specify on a map. A standard printout from the computer of census figures covering the topics needed in Appendix F costs about $90. Those who are interested in this source should contact: Center for Social Research in the Church, Box 75-K, Concordia Teachers College, 7400 Augusta Street, River Forest, IL 60305.

The 1970 U.S. Census was reported in several series, each of which consists of fifty-eight parts. Part one gives summary figures for the United States. Parts two through fifty-two give figures for the fifty states and the District of Columbia in alphabetical order. Parts fifty-three through fifty-eight do the same for Puerto Rico, Guam, the Virgin Islands, American Samoa, and the Trust Territory of the Pacific Islands, respectively.

Series PC(1)-A* is titled: *Number of Inhabitants.* This volume contains final population counts for each state, each county in the state, each Standard Metropolitan Statistical Area (SMSA), each urbanized area, and for *all* county subdivisions, incorporated places, and unincorporated places of 1,000 inhabitants or more. Maps showing the various subdivisions, places, towns, and urbanized areas are also found in this volume.

Series PC(1)-B is titled: *General Population Characteristics.* This volume presents statistics on age, sex, race, marital status, and relationship to the head of the household for the state, for counties by urban and rural residence, for SMSAs, for urbanized areas, for county subdivisions, and for places of 1,000 inhabitants or more.

Series PC(1)-C is titled: *General Social and Economic Characteristics.* This volume presents statistics on: nativity and parentage, state or country of birth, Spanish origin, mother tongue, residence five years ago, year moved into present house, school enrollment (public or private), years of school completed, vocational training, number of children ever born, family composition, disability, veteran status, employment status, place of work, means of transportation to work, occupation group, industry group, class of worker, and income (by type) in 1969 of families and individuals. Each of these subjects is shown for some or all of the following areas: the state, counties (by urban, rural-nonfarm, and rural-farm residence), SMSAs, urbanized areas, and places of 2,500 inhabitants or more.

Series HC(1)-A is titled: *General Housing Characteristics.* This volume presents statistics on: tenure, kitchen facilities, plumbing facilities, number of rooms, persons

---

* U.S. Government code uses PC for "population census," HC for "housing census," and PHC for census books which include both "population and housing census" data.

per room, units in structure, mobile home, telephone, value, contract rent, and vacancy status for the state (by urban and rural residence), for SMSAs, for urbanized areas, for places of 1,000 inhabitants or more, and counties.

Series HC(1)-B is titled: *Detailed Housing Characteristics.* This volume presents statistics on a more detailed basis than the preceding volume and also on the subjects of: year moved into unit, year structure was built, basement, heating equipment, fuels, air conditioning, water and sewage, appliances, gross rent, and ownership of second home. Each subject is shown for some or all of the following areas: the state (by urban, rural-nonfarm, and rural-farm residence), SMSAs, urbanized areas, places of 2,500 inhabitants or more, and counties.

In addition to these volumes reporting facts for each state as divided into smaller geographical units, there is a set of reports available for the Standard Metropolitan Statistical Areas (SMSAs). This set of reports shows data for most of the population and housing subjects included in the 1970 Census.

Facts are reported for each census tract. Census tracts are the small areas into which large cities and their adjacent areas have been divided for statistical purposes. Except in New England, a Standard Metropolitan Statistical Area is a county or group of counties next to each other which contains at least one city of 50,000 inhabitants or more, or twin cities with a combined population of at least 50,000. In addition to the county or counties containing such a city or cities, counties next to each other are included in an SMSA if, according to certain criteria, they are socially and economically integrated with the central city. In New England, SMSAs consist of towns and cities instead of counties.

WHERE TO LOOK FOR THE FACTS YOU NEED—Nonmetropolitan Churches

First, use the maps found in *PC(1)-A* (state name), *Number of Inhabitants* to help you decide what is your *area* and your *neighborhood;* follow suggestions provided on page 193 of Appendix F. After you have decided what village, town, city (or groups of such minor civil divisions) to use in defining your *neighborhood* and your *area,* you are ready to look up the various tables in the census reports. The reports are organized by population size. Therefore, the first step in making use of the various tables is to determine the population category for your *neighborhood* and your *area.* For this purpose, use Table 6 of *PC(1)-A* (state name), *Number of Inhabitants.* You may have to list several units together and then place the total in the appropriate place on page 193 of Appendix F. If for your *area* you are using your county, you will find the 1970 total county population reported in the second column of Table 9 in that same volume.

The remaining instructions for completing pages 193 through 205 of Appendix F are organized according to the specific items requested.

	10,000–50,000 population	2,500–10,000 population	1,000–2,500 population	County Subdivisions	Counties
	Table	Table	Table	Table	Table
Page 193 of Appendix F					
items 1-4[1]	27	31	32	33	34
item 5[2]	41	42	n.a.[3]	n.a.	44
item 6[2]	40	42	n.a.	n.a.	43
Page 195 of Appendix F					

to be used to accumulate figures from several places, using tables as above.

	10,000–50,000	2,500–10,000	1,000–2,500	County Subdiv.	Counties
Page 197 of Appendix F					
entire page[2]	105	118	n.a.	n.a.	122
Page 199 of Appendix F					
entire page[1]	28	31	n.a.	n.a.	35

[1] Table is located in *PC(1)-B* (state name) *General Population Characteristics.*
[2] Table is located in *PC(1)-C* (state name) *General Social and Economic Characteristics.*
[3] Not Available.

	10,000–50,000	2,500–10,000	1,000–2,500	County Subdiv.	Counties
Page 205 of Appendix F					
items 2-5[4]	18	23	27	n.a.	29
item 6	19	23	n.a.	n.a.	60
item 7	20	24	27	n.a.	29
item 8[5]	53	58	27	n.a.	62
items 9-15	53	58	n.a.	n.a.	62
item 16	54	58	27	n.a.	62

[4] Tables 18-29 are located in *HC(1)-A* (state name) *General Housing Characteristics.*
[5] Tables 53-62 are located in *HC(1)-B* (state name) *Detailed Housing Characteristics.*

WHERE TO LOOK FOR THE FACTS YOU NEED—Metropolitan Churches

First, use the map found in *PHC(1)* No. (your metropolitan area name) *Census Tracts* to help you decide which census tracts you will use for your *neighborhood* and which for your *area* (may be an entire city). You will particularly want to use page 195 of Appendix F to organize your data as reported on page 193 and to make a record of the census tracts which you are using. Note also that some figures needed for Appendix F pages are not available in these census tract reports. They can be found at the level of your city or town using the guidelines provided in the section for nonmetropolitan churches above. Tables reported below are to be found in the PHC *Census Tracts* report.

Appendix F Page	Item	PHC Table	Item Name
193	1	P-1	Race—All Persons
	2	P-1	Race—White
	3	P-1	Race—Negro
	4	n.a.	
	5	P-4	All Families—Median Income
	6	P-2	Years of School Completed—Median School Years Completed
197	all but last	P-3	Occupation—Total Employed
	last	P-3	Occupation—Female Employed
199	all	P-1	Age by Sex—Male/Female
205	2	H-1	All Housing Units
	3	H-1	Tenure, Race, and Vacancy Status—Owner Occupied
	4	H-1	Tenure, Race, and Vacancy Status—Renter Occupied
	5	H-1	Lacking Some or All Plumbing Facilities—All Units
	6	H-1	Persons—Median, All Occupied Units
	7	H-1	Value—Median
	8-12	H-2	Units in Structure
	13-15	H-2	Year Structure Built (Be sure to combine items as needed)
	16	H-2	Gross Rent—Median

ADDITIONAL FACTS WHICH MAY INTEREST YOU

As you get the figures required on pages 193 through 205 of Appendix F, you may also see other items in the census reports which interest you. In some communities, it will be important to know about the ethnic backgrounds of the population. See: *PC(1)-C* (state name) *General Social and Economic Characteristics.* More detailed information about the Hispanic population is provided in separate tables throughout if the Spanish-speaking population is relatively large. You may want to discover whether persons work within your county or work elsewhere; what proportion of the population is married, single, or divorced. You may want facts about the "poverty" population. All of these items are in the census reports.

AN IMPORTANT CAUTION

Be sure that the figures you copy into Appendix F are correct. Check the column heading and your place in the table of the census report. With a long series of numbers in the census reports, it is easy to find yourself copying figures for a different item or a different town. Take a few moments to study the categories used in a table of the census report to ensure that you have actually copied the figures you wanted.

INTERVIEWING COMMUNITY LEADERS

WHO AND WHAT TO ASK

Each community is different. The titles held by community leaders are different. The employment base is different. Community attitudes also differ from place to place. However, every community has persons in leadership positions. These leaders should know what is happening in and to the community. Interviewing such leaders is an important way of gathering information about a community.

The following pages describe fifty possible types of leaders. The various parts of community life are divided into categories, such as: education, government, business, and industry. *You do not need to interview every type of leader suggested in these pages, but you should try to see persons from each of the categories.*

Some questions should be included in every interview. Other questions will be "tailor-made" to a specific leader because of his/her responsibility. Additional help concerning interview techniques can be found in "Since You Must Ask" by Lawrence Janssen.*

Questions to Be Asked in Every Interview

- What is your name and position? (If not already known.)

- What do you feel are the most critical needs, problems, or issues in your community?

- What kind of response do you see the community making to each of these needs?

- What role do you feel churches of the community are taking?

- What image do you have of＿＿＿＿＿?
  (name your church)

- In what way(s) can your church be helpful to you in your responsibilities?

Questions Which Might Be Asked in Any Interview

- How long have you held your present position? (Such information helps you in asking other questions. For example, a person who came to a position six months ago is usually less able to describe detailed facts about what happened two years earlier.)

- What do you particularly like about this community? Or, what about this community makes you particularly glad to live/work here?

- What about this community do you wish could be changed?

*Order "Action Guide 16" from: National Ministries Literature, American Baptist Churches in the U.S.A., Valley Forge, PA 19481 (Price: 25¢ per copy plus postage.)

EDUCATION

1. *Principal of the nearest elementary school:* Unless many students are bused from distant neighborhoods, the elementary school usually reflects most clearly the characteristics of its neighborhood. The principal usually knows children personally and has a feeling for their home backgrounds. Some questions for the principal are:

   a. What is the current enrollment of your school?

   b. In the last five (or ten) years what has been the trend of this enrollment?

   c. What future enrollment do you project for this school and what factors will cause any changes?

   d. What has been your mobility rate (children moving from or to the school) in the last year? What factors have caused this rate?

   e. Which minorities are in the school? What is the proportion of the total enrollment for each? What is the trend of minority group enrollment?

   f. What impressions do you have about the family background of the children in this school? What percentage of the children have both parents employed? What percentage are from one-parent families? What percentage are in economic poverty (or, how many are on a government-supported lunch program)?

   g. How well does the community support its schools? What acceptance do tax levies or school bonds have in the community?

h. Do you provide special education classes? For what kinds of handicaps or special needs? How many are involved? Do you feel there are persons not being reached by special education opportunities?

i. Have you developed any particular educational innovations? What are they? How well do you feel they are working?

j. Do you offer a hot lunch program? Do the children have to go home for lunch? If they go home, how many have an adult at home?

k. What type of recreational program is offered through the schools? How are the school building and the playground used after school hours and in the summer?

l. Have there been budget cuts which affected staff, extra curricular program, field trips, music, art, athletics? What is your evaluation of the effect of these cuts on the children?

m. What are some of your personal concerns for the children of the community? For the schools? For the community?

2. *Principal of nearby junior high school:* You would likely ask many of the same questions as listed above. You could also ask about the programs in sex education, moral or religious values, athletics, ethnic or minority group identity and history.

3. *Principal of nearby high school:* Many of the questions described above remain helpful at the high school level. In addition you may want to ask about student government, interscholastic athletics, dropout rates, the proportion of seniors going on to further education, and impressions about what proportion of high school graduates leave the community.

You could also ask about educational offerings for students who are interested in vocational-technical goals and about how the school handles the variety of interests students bring to the school. For example, are gifted students provided accelerated courses? The principal should also have a feeling about work opportunities and recreational opportunities for teenagers. You may

also want to ask about impressions concerning drug abuse, alcohol consumption, smoking, and teenage pregnancies.

4. *Student leaders at nearby high school:* You might work out such an interview with the principal and meet with students during a lunch hour. What are the impressions of such leaders as the student body president or the high school newspaper editor about the school and the community? What are the critical issues as they see them? What changes in school policy are they seeking? Do they receive support or resistance from school officials when, as student leaders, they represent student opinion about issues?

5. *Superintendent of schools:* From this person should come an overview of the public school system and its needs, accomplishments, goals, frustrations, and opportunities. Broad information about enrollment trends, ethnic and minority enrollment, special education, and continuing and adult education should be available. Policies about use of school property for the recreational and cultural needs of the community (the community schools plan) need to be revealed. What plans does the system have for new school construction? Are major changes planned in school policies?

6. *Director of Continuing or Adult Education for high school or community college.* Ask about degree and non-degree programs offered; enrollment trends; availability of off-campus courses for interested groups.

7. *President, dean, or other leader at nearby college:* Enrollment trends and projections, background of student body, particular programs being offered, town-gown relationships, needs of students or faculty and administration, how the college can be a resource to the community, expansion plans for the campus are topics for some of the questions to be asked. Also find out what proportion of students live on-campus, in the community, or commute. (Commuting students normally find themselves less involved in campus-related activities.)

8. *College student leaders:* Presidents of the student body and the newspaper editor could be interviewed together about issues as listed above in #4. Community attitudes, work

opportunities, and openings for volunteer service should be explored.

GOVERNMENT

9. *City or county manager:* When your community has such a person, he/she has the responsibility of coordinating the administrative services offered by the governmental unit. Some questions for the manager are:

   a. What is the present population for your community (city, village, county)?

   b. What is the trend of population change and what is projected for the future? What primary factors contribute to this trend?

   c. How adequate are such community resources as water, electricity, sewage disposal, solid waste disposal, etc.?

   d. What are the primary forms of employment in your community? Are these changing?

   e. Are changes expected in the way land is used in your community?

   f. How healthy is your central business district (or downtown)? How adequate is off-street parking? What proportion of storefronts are vacant?

   g. What services in your community are most effective?

   h. What services for your community are least effective?

   i. What citizen groups are heard the most in your office? What are their concerns?

10. *Mayor:* Even in communities which have a city manager, the mayor can be a very influential individual. Mayors can be asked many or all of the same questions asked of city managers. In addition, inquire about the political climate. How much agreement or disagreement is there in the community about what its major needs are and how these should be met? Who (by name) are the major leaders and opinion makers of your community?

11. *City council member, selectperson, supervisor, commissioner:* Persons elected to public office either represent voters of a part of the community or represent "at-large" catego-

ries. (In either case they had to take their views and opinions to the voters.) Probe with such persons their views about government services, community life, and the "health" of the community.

12. *City or county planner:* Many of the questions asked of the city manager apply to the planner also. This person should have important information about population trends and projections, land use, zoning, where growth (if any) will occur, the nature of residential or commercial development, trends of the church's specific neighborhood, housing patterns and availability. The planner can be asked about ecological concerns for the total environment.

13. *Employment Service (government) official:* You will want to know about employment and unemployment in your community, the type of employment available, the proportion of women in the labor force, impressions about needs in day care, stability of local industries and businesses, economic and job projections, etc.

14. *Welfare case worker or official:* Welfare includes financial aid and other services. Financial aid includes federally subsidized programs (Aid to Families of Dependent Children, Aid to the Blind, Aid to the Disabled, Old Age Assistance) and local and state supported programs (general assistance). You should find out how many cases (and persons) are represented in each category, what the trends for each category are, and how close financial support comes to actual living costs. How many cases does each case worker have? What are the other services being provided? What proportion of the need does each service reach?

15. *Urban Renewal or Rural Development official:* Seek information about the physical changes which have been achieved and which are proposed. What has happened to persons and families who were displaced? Probe the moral implications of the means used and the goals (ends) being sought in renewal and development efforts.

16. *Housing authority official:* You will want to find out what kind of low-income housing there is and how much has been developed in your community. How long must eligible persons wait for such housing? How many

are on the waiting list? Has your community provided housing for low-income families? The elderly? Is there a community room in one or more of the housing projects? If so, what use is made of it? What community groups could offer programs in the housing project?

17. *County extension agent:* County agents are a key contact about agricultural trends, land use, services to children, youth, homemakers, and older adults. Programs in nutrition, 4-H, or FFA can be explored. The relationships among other people-serving agencies and the quality of their services are often clearly seen by the county agent.

18. *Parks and recreation official:* Speak with a person involved with planning for parks and open space, programming for recreational needs of all ages, and preparing the budget requests for these programs. Playgrounds, gymnasiums, swimming pools, cultural centers, community centers, and parks represent the kind of public space for recreation every community might desire. What does yours have? How adequate are these facilities? Who can use them? What age groups receive most attention? What age groups are left out of planning and programming?

19. *Environmental Resources official:* What are the environmental standards governing your community's quality for air, water, solid waste, noise, and population density? What kind of exceptions to these standards are being permitted in Environmental Impact Statements? In what ways are citizens of your community involved in creating these standards and in enforcing them?

20. *Transportation official:* What are the available services in public transportation? What are current plans for increasing such services? What alternatives to automotive transportation are under consideration? Has your community tried to develop new forms of mass transit? What happened as a result? What do you feel is the public attitude toward mass transit? How well does traffic flow in and around your community? What changes in traffic flow are expected? What highways will be developed?

21. *Law enforcement officer:* A police chief can reflect on the entire range of crime and legal violations to be found in the community. A juvenile officer can focus more specifically on the forms that delinquency or juvenile dependency takes in your community. Drug abuse, alcoholism, shoplifting; police-community relationships; and specific services, such as the Police Athletic League, should be explored.

22. *Local judge:* This person usually has a perspective on the overall crime picture, the backlog in the criminal justice system, and on drug abuse, vandalism, and shoplifting. The present forms of judicial process, overall law enforcement, effectiveness of various institutions to which offenders and dependents are sent, and the probation system are other important topics to explore.

23. *Planning commission member:* Seek from this person the amount of information available to him/her as a nonprofessional in planning and his/her attitudes or concerns which influence public planning policy.

24. *Human relations commission member:* Explore whether the commission is only a "complaint" board which takes actions to better racial relationships when pushed to do so. Or, is it a board which initiates programs in the community? You may want to find out if the commission puts all of its efforts into race relations or if it also probes issues of sex orientation and age-group differences.

BUSINESS AND INDUSTRY

25. *Chamber of commerce official:* Chamber executives are responsible for public relations, services to tourists, stimulation of local business, industrial and community development, etc. These persons should know about the business climate, including the proportion of shopping done locally as opposed to that done in a nearby major city. Many questions asked of other persons about community life are appropriate for chamber officials.

26. *Local realtor:* Ask about trends of the persons who are moving into and out of the community. Where is new development taking place or where can it be expected soon? What are the trends in land value and land use? What is happening in terms of single family dwellings and multi-family

dwellings? What impressions do you have about specific neighborhoods of our community? How much housing is available for low and middle-income families? What are the trends in tax rates?

27. *Local banker:* A banker can share retail business trends, housing trends, population trends, economic trends, and projections for future growth and development. Inquire about what is happening to the neighborhood of the church.

28. *Local retailer:* A person in business often has information about the neighborhood, the kind of people with whom he/she does business, changes in attitude of the public, as well as specific information about trends and projections for retail sales.

29. *Tourism related person:* An owner or manager of a resort, campground, motel, or other tourist-related attraction/business can provide you information about visitors to your community. Where are people coming from? How long do they stay? What other services in the community do they ask about?

30. *Industrial leader:* An official of your community's leading industry should be able to help you learn how stable the employment base has been and is going to be. You can find out about labor-management relations, community attitudes toward this industry, whether the industry encourages its executives to be involved in the community, the economic outlook for the community, the industry's approach to equal employment opportunities and to environmental concerns.

31. *Labor union official:* If your community has a union that has strong influence, see one of its officials. Ask the union official about wage scales, working conditions, labor-management relations, safety on the job, the union's influence on the community, and its employment projections for the next few years.

32. *Grange leader:* Ask such persons about local agricultural trends and concerns as well as what types of services are being provided through the Grange and other farmer-oriented agencies.

33. *Service station manager:* Inquire about the neighborhood and what kind of changes have taken place over the span of several years.

COMMUNICATIONS

34. *Newspaper editor:* How extensive is the paper's circulation and what is its editorial policy about local issues? What provision does the paper make to cover all ethnic groups in the community? What is the policy of the paper about religious news? Does the paper see itself as having a role in mobilizing citizen support for key local issues?

35. *Radio-TV executive:* What is the station's range of influence and its editorial policy for dealing with local issues? How is public service time now being used? What can churches do to use mass communications better? What is the executive's evaluation of the community?

36. *Cable television manager:* How accessible is a cable TV channel for community programming or for church programming? Ask similar questions to those asked of newspaper and radio-TV people.

SOCIAL SERVICE AGENCIES

37. *Council of Social Agencies executive:* This person should know about the range of social services in the community and have a good grasp of the needs. Inquire what studies have been done in the community by other agencies and whether reports from these studies are available. Secure, if possible, a listing of the social service agencies available in your community.

38. *Community Mental Health director:* Explore the case load for the mental health center and the waiting time between contact and actually receiving service. What age groups show up most in the patient population and what seems to be the focus of their illnesses or needs? How does the center relate to other community agencies? How strong is the preventive aspect of the center's program?

39. *Health official:* How adequate are hospital services (including emergency room treatment)? What is the ratio of doctors to the population served? What is being done in terms of preventative medicine and the use of paraprofessionals? What is the official's evaluation of your community's drug-abuse programs, halfway houses, or other special services?

40. *Family counselor:* Explore family relationship trends, family tensions, styles of family life, broken homes, adequacy of other services for family units and single adults.

41. *Community fund director:* United Fund or the community fund-raising effort usually involves many persons from the community. In larger communities it may also involve paid staff. Such persons often have information about the community, the effectiveness of various agencies and programs, and unmet needs.

42. *Child care staff:* These persons should know your community's need for child care programs, preschool programs, nursery school, extended care, etc. They can also share what is now being offered.

43. *Older adult staff:* Persons working in programs with senior citizens and the senior citizen leaders themselves can provide information about the needs and concerns of older adults in the community. Housing, nutrition, transportation, group facilities and programs, employment, and health care are some of the topics which need to be explored as each relates to older adults. Also explore the present and potential volunteer service opportunities for older adults of your community.

44. *Representative of nearby institutions:* Explore the role such institutions have in your community and how your community relates to these institutions. Included among these are: retirement homes, prisons, nursing homes, mental hospitals, state schools, YMCAs, YWCAs, halfway houses, children's homes, etc.

OTHER LEADERS

45. *Pastor of nearby church:* Discover what is happening in and through his/her church. Ask about such things as trends in membership and attendance. Many questions asked of persons in other positions can also be asked of pastors.

46. *Local council of churches executive:* A paid or volunteer executive for a cooperating organization of churches usually is able to share information about churches doing creative programming. Explore what forms cooperative ministry is taking and what might be done.

47. *Minority or ethnic group representative:* Persons and organizations representing minority groups can share valuable insights regarding their concerns and how they perceive community attitudes. Blacks, Hispanics, Native-Americans, Asian-Americans, or other ethnic groups should be considered, including such groups as Southern Christian Leadership Movement, Urban League, and the American Indian Movement.

48. *Conservation or ecology organization representative:* Ask about efforts being made to protect wildlife, to meet issues of land use and ecology, to improve the quality of life.

49. *Neighborhood homemaker:* A homemaker who lives near your church can share important opinions on community services, local issues, images about the churches and family life. The homemaker can give you another consumer's attitude toward schools, retail stores, social service agencies, and governmental services.

50. *Losing candidate for major public office:* In many cases, a losing candidate in a recent election can provide perspectives and insights regarding the community which would be hard to get from current officeholders.

WORLD DATA

The following questions should be answered by your Planning Task Force and by others who can give representative church opinions.

1. In its annual budget, does your church include an amount for international missions? ☐ Yes ☐ No.

   What percentage is this of your total budget? _____ %

2. List events within other countries which you feel may have a direct influence on your church's outreach or service ministries (i.e., food shortages, inflation, energy, unemployment, war, etc.)

Country	Event	Implications for Your Church
_____	_____	_____
_____	_____	_____
_____	_____	_____

3. What do you feel are the six critical issues in today's world? (Consider such things as: world peace, adequate food supplies, overpopulation, refugees, etc.)

   1. _____
   2. _____
   3. _____
   4. _____
   5. _____
   6. _____

4. Has your church taken specific action in response to any of these issues? List each issue and identify your response.

Issue	Response
_____	_____
_____	_____
_____	_____
_____	_____

5. If there are critical issues on which your church has not yet acted, which one(s) do you feel you should work on next? List in order of priority.

_____

_____

_____

_____

6. Which group in your church carries the main responsibility to study world problems and to help your congregation respond?

_____

7. What sources does your congregation use to become familiar with world issues?

_____

8. To what degree are your Planning Task Force and your congregation aware of your denomination's involvement in world problems and issues?

_____

9. List specific instances for which your church is especially supportive of your denomination's involvement in world problems and needs.

_____

_____

_____

10. Has your church ever communicated with a member of the United States Congress or with the U.S. President to express its feelings about global concerns (such as the release of U.S. grain for world use, American military involvement overseas, atomic warfare, etc.)? List each and include dates.

The Issue Communicated   **When**

_____   _____

_____   _____

_____   _____

11. Has your church ever communicated with your denominational leadership about its specific concerns over international problems? List each concern and identify to whom the communication was sent.

The Issue Communicated   **To Whom?**

_____   _____

_____   _____

_____   _____

12. Which groups in your church could help your congregation respond to worldwide needs (i.e., youth, men, women, small groups, etc.)?

   _____   _____

   _____   _____

   _____   _____

13. Are international concerns made a matter of prayer in your morning worship service? □ Yes □ No. If "yes," how often? Weekly □; At least monthly □; Less often □ .

WATCH OUT!
VERBS CONTROL OBJECTIVES

Follow five principles as you select the verb for each objective.

Read each principle. Then check over the list of verbs given as examples. Finally, look at the recommendation.

When you write objectives:

1. Avoid verbs which point to an outcome beyond the ability of the planner to achieve. Some of these verbs are:

   request
   invite
   persuade
   offer

   RECOMMENDATION: Don't use these verbs.

2. Avoid verbs which describe a process but *not* the outcome for which the process is undertaken. Some of these verbs are:

   seek
   try to
   survey
   discuss
   review
   continue
   grow
   deepen
   advance
   serve
   encourage
   influence

   RECOMMENDATION: Press for the verb which gives the reason *why* behind the process verb. Example: "Try to recruit three persons . . ." becomes "Enlist three persons. . . ."

3. Avoid verbs which express results so vague that people cannot agree on what is meant.

   appreciate
   understand
   know

   RECOMMENDATION: Don't use these verbs.

4. Avoid verbs which are limited to thinking rather than acting.

   investigate
   study
   examine
   think about
   consider

   RECOMMENDATION: Save these verbs for first steps in your Program Plans.

5. Avoid verbs which express change *unless* you clearly state your starting point, the time period to be used, *and* the amount of change you want.

   increase
   deepen
   enhance
   preserve
   support
   maintain
   decrease
   reduce

   RECOMMENDATION: Be sure you specify your starting point, the time period needed, and the amount of change you want. Example: "Increase our visiting teams" becomes "Increase our visiting teams from two teams to four teams in six months."

WHY PLANS FAIL*

Central to improving how you plan is finding out why some plans fail. It is simple enough: discover what contributes to failure and what must be done to reduce the possibility of failure. Failure is a certainty if you don't work hard, but simply working harder is not enough. Working smarter is essential. You can work smarter by learning from seven basic reasons why plans fail.

1. *No Real Goals* . . . therefore, no *real* plan. If there is no plan, the plan can't fail, but you can. Oddly enough many goal-setters don't actually know what a real goal is. They may point to some ideal mission such as "improve," "grow," or "increase ministry," but words this vague result in fantasies instead of goals. If your goal statement does not describe a condition or an end-state you want, it is *not* a goal.

2. *No Measurable Objectives.* If you don't know just what you intend to do, you will never know if you did it. Objectives are the guides to action. They must contain "action" verbs; without such action there will be little movement toward goal accomplishment. Objectives must be stated so they are measurable.

3. *Failure to Anticipate Obstacles.* No one can think of every contingency. Rash enthusiasm hampers a sensible effort to take account of possible obstacles and pitfalls. Every plan, no matter how carefully prepared, has limitations and built-in conflicts over priorities and resources. Planners who identify possible obstacles and ways to overcome them have superior batting averages. Effective planners take what at first they perceive to be large obstacles and break them down into small hurdles. They then develop ways to overcome each one. In short, a plan should be flexible enough to handle obstacles, whether anticipated or not.

4. *Lack of Milestones for Progress Reviews.* Plans that fail often have no concrete milestones or dates to review progress. Or milestones are allowed to slip by unnoticed. Famous last words in planning include: "It can wait," "I can remember that," or "I know how I'm doing." Periodic reviews of progress can alert you to the need for adjusting your plans or even your objectives. Milestones reached provide an important sense of accomplishment and desire to succeed further. Effective progress reviews provide a test of direction and pace. They also provide a check on the reality of the plan as you move along.

5. *Lack of Commitment.* Personal commitment is critical to the success of any plan. Laity may be hindered in long-range planning without a personal commitment from the pastor to support the process; the reverse is also true. Commitment means the willingness to see a plan through to completion. Commitment is stimulated by taking part in developing goals and objectives. Involve as many persons as possible in the goal and objective writing process.

6. *Failure to Revise Objectives.* A sure way to torpedo the best-laid plan is failure to restudy and reset objectives when indicated by new facts. Failure results when plans are not flexible enough to respond to changes in circumstances. It is important to rewrite objectives when necessary.

7. *Failure to Learn from Experience.* Failure to learn from experience arises when planners are unwilling to change their way of doing things. Many take comfort in the thought: "It's worked before; therefore it must be right." This attitude, however, will prevent you from ever finding out if "it is right" for this time until it is too late.

Summary

Learning how to plan is easy. Learning how to prevent plans from failing is difficult. The seven basic reasons why plans fail are shown in the chart. The symptoms which signal their presence and some of the best cures now available are also shown.

*Adapted from *New Venture Creation* by Jeffry A. Timmons; Leonard E. Smollen; and Alexander L. M. Dingee, Jr. (Homewood, Ill.: Richard D. Irwin, Inc., 1977), chapter 6; used with the authors' permission.

PLANNING: ITS REASONS FOR FAILURE, SYMPTOMS, AND CURES

REASONS FOR FAILURE	SYMPTOMS	CURES
1) No Real Goals	• Do not reflect the church's purpose statement • Talk about program plans • Are vague—sound good; say little • Completely beyond the reach of the church • Not "owned" by membership	• Relate goal to purpose statement • Rewrite goals so they describe end-states you want to reach or conditions you want to bring about • Involve more persons in goal writing
2) No Measurable Objectives	• Are not related to a goal • Are not measurable, specific, or time-phased • Do not contain action verbs	• Build each objective from a goal • Answer in objectives such questions as: Who? How many? Where? When? • Identify short term and long term objectives • Use action verbs in the statement
3) Failure to Anticipate Obstacles	• Excessive optimism • Closing your eyes to conflicts • Completion dates not met • "Ooops, I forgot!" • Didn't get support when needed • Crises are common	• Take time to list possible obstacles • Prepare ways to overcome listed obstacles • Be realistic in setting dates • Check Program Plan Details • Talk to Program Plan Manager • Revise Program Plan or Details
4) Lack of Milestones and Progress Reviews	• Completion dates not set • "It can wait," "I can remember that" • "Let's play this by ear" • Don't really know how you are doing • Everything is short-term; no long-term aspects • Don't remember when the last review took place • No plans revised recently	• Set specific task milestones; stick to them • See that the Program Plan Manager is on the job • Review your progress on the dates set • Ask the question: Are we making enough progress toward the objective?

5) Lack of Commitment	• Putting things off • Just doing daily, routine activities • "I don't care what happens" • Have not set priorities • Planners skip meetings • No reports submitted • Pastor or lay members don't "own" the plan	• Involve others in the planning process • Share proposed plans early so new ideas can influence their development • Give the small groups of your church a chance to discuss proposed plans • Talk with each team member to find out the level of his/her commitment • Recruit replacements, as necessary • Celebrate successes you've had
6) Failure to Revise Objectives	• Plans never change • Being inflexible, refusing to face new facts that call for change • No sense of movement toward objectives • Help not sought when needed • Waste time on programs that don't work • Programs don't fit your priorities	• Deliberately seek feedback • Compare feedback with your standards for achieving the objective • Change emphasis and approach when it is appropriate • Encourage Program Plan Managers to alert Planning Task Force when revision is needed • Review progress more often
7) Failure to Learn from Experience	• Lose sight of goals • Repeat mistakes • Feedback is ignored • Evaluation standards are not used • Face the same crisis again and again • Unwillingness to change ways of doing things • Never asking, "What did we learn this time?"	• Use milestones to review progress • Have program units, task forces, etc., meet with the Planning Task Force • Keep a record of changes made as a result of evaluation • Concentrate on results, not on giving reports for their own sake

ROLE EXPECTATIONS CHECKLIST*

"The origin of this form is unknown. I received a shorter version from the Rt. Rev. John R. Wyatt, Episcopal bishop of Spokane, who found it being used in one of his churches. I have expanded and revised it, reworked the questions for easy scoring, and have used it many times."

—Paul Beeman

PURPOSE:

A mutual understanding of the role which a minister takes and the roles taken by the church members can do much to improve the effectiveness of a church. This checklist is designed to help each person look at what he/she expects of lay members and of the pastor. Each answer expresses a personal feeling. There are no right or wrong answers. Sharing answers among church members and the minister can start a fruitful discussion that leads to mutual goals and expectations.

EXPECTATIONS OF THE PASTOR. In your opinion what should demand the greatest amount of time, thought, and preparation? What should have priority over other activities on the pastor's schedule? Enter your priority ratings for pastors by *circling* the appropriate number for each item.

EXPECTATIONS OF CHURCH MEMBERS. In your opinion what should demand the greatest amount of time, thought, and preparation? What should have priority over other activities for the members of your church? Enter your priority ratings for church members by *underlining* the appropriate number for each item.

	Priority	
	low	high
1. Relates to sick, dying, and bereaved persons.	10 9 8 7 6 5 4 3 2 1	
2. Maintains a disciplined life of prayer and personal devotion.	10 9 8 7 6 5 4 3 2 1	
3. Teaches or works directly with Christian education classes in church school or Bible school.	10 9 8 7 6 5 4 3 2 1	
4. Does church office work, typing, mimeographing, record-keeping.	10 9 8 7 6 5 4 3 2 1	
5. Understands how groups work well and helps church groups and organizations function efficiently.	10 9 8 7 6 5 4 3 2 1	
6. Visits in the homes of church members.	10 9 8 7 6 5 4 3 2 1	
7. Participates in denominational activities beyond the local church, district, conference or regional work.	10 9 8 7 6 5 4 3 2 1	
8. Seeks to locate needy persons and families in the community.	10 9 8 7 6 5 4 3 2 1	

*Adapted from: *The Interpreter*, Program Journal of The United Methodist Church, vol. 18, no. 5 (May, 1974).

	Priority	
	low	high

9. Participates personally in community projects and organizations (such as school board, PTA, United Fund Campaign).

10 9 8 7 6 5 4 3 2 1

10. Seeks to bring about constructive social change and community improvement.

10 9 8 7 6 5 4 3 2 1

11. Leads or assists in public worship.

10 9 8 7 6 5 4 3 2 1

12. Reads and studies the Bible.

10 9 8 7 6 5 4 3 2 1

13. Teaches special courses or adult study groups.

10 9 8 7 6 5 4 3 2 1

14. Works on (or with) church board and committees.

10 9 8 7 6 5 4 3 2 1

15. Tries to identify and resolve conflict among church members and leaders.

10 9 8 7 6 5 4 3 2 1

16. Calls on new residents and prospective members.

10 9 8 7 6 5 4 3 2 1

17. Interprets and implements denominational programs within the local church.

10 9 8 7 6 5 4 3 2 1

18. Personally assists victims of fire, flood, injury, injustice, neglect, or unemployment.

10 9 8 7 6 5 4 3 2 1

19. Represents the church in local organizations (such as Chamber of Commerce, YMCA, Council of Churches).

10 9 8 7 6 5 4 3 2 1

20. Identifies who are victims of social neglect, injustice, discrimination, or prejudice, and helps bring them to public attention.

10 9 8 7 6 5 4 3 2 1

21. Studies for, writes, and preaches sermons.

10 9 8 7 6 5 4 3 2 1

22. Cultivates a personal social life outside of church activities.

10 9 8 7 6 5 4 3 2 1

23. Works with church young people in classes or fellowship groups.

10 9 8 7 6 5 4 3 2 1

24. Works on (or with) church budget, finance drive, and building campaign.

10 9 8 7 6 5 4 3 2 1

25. Leads or helps the church in the process of setting its goals.

10 9 8 7 6 5 4 3 2 1

26. Talks with persons about their spiritual development, religious life, and beliefs.

10 9 8 7 6 5 4 3 2 1

27. Explains home and foreign missionary work and promotes financial support from church members.

10 9 8 7 6 5 4 3 2 1

28. Encourages church members to help persons in need by contributions, counseling, and tutoring.

10 9 8 7 6 5 4 3 2 1

29. Seeks to involve church members in program to help others through organizations (such as

| | Priority | |
| | low | high |

YWCA, Indian Center, groups for older persons).   10 9 8 7 6 5 4 3 2 1

30. Testifies before city council or state legislature committees to correct or improve unjust ordinances or laws.   10 9 8 7 6 5 4 3 2 1

31. Counsels people about personal and moral problems and about major decisions of life, such as marriage or vocation.   10 9 8 7 6 5 4 3 2 1

32. Maintains prayer and devotions in the family circle.   10 9 8 7 6 5 4 3 2 1

33. Serves as summer camp counselor.   10 9 8 7 6 5 4 3 2 1

34. Recruits and trains church program and organization leaders.   10 9 8 7 6 5 4 3 2 1

35. Seeks to maintain openness among church leaders and members.   10 9 8 7 6 5 4 3 2 1

36. Finds ways to witness for Christ in daily life contacts with people.   10 9 8 7 6 5 4 3 2 1

37. Serves as an example by generously donating to church benevolences.   10 9 8 7 6 5 4 3 2 1

38. Seeks to understand the special needs of minority groups, such as Indians, Blacks, Asians, migrants.   10 9 8 7 6 5 4 3 2 1

39. Is an active member of a service club (such as Rotary, Lions).   10 9 8 7 6 5 4 3 2 1

40. Speaks before church, community, and civic groups, on radio or TV, regarding problems and needs in the community.   10 9 8 7 6 5 4 3 2 1

41. Provides for baptisms, Communion, weddings, and funerals.   10 9 8 7 6 5 4 3 2 1

42. Serves as an example of higher than average moral and ethical character.   10 9 8 7 6 5 4 3 2 1

43. Conducts or assists in church membership or confirmation classes for youth and adults.   10 9 8 7 6 5 4 3 2 1

44. Supplies main ideas and sets directions for the church.   10 9 8 7 6 5 4 3 2 1

45. Leads or helps in evaluating the past year's programs.   10 9 8 7 6 5 4 3 2 1

46. Seeks the commitment of persons to the Christian life and to church activities.   10 9 8 7 6 5 4 3 2 1

47. Promotes interchurch cooperation in the community.   10 9 8 7 6 5 4 3 2 1

48. Organizes church programs to assist persons in need.   10 9 8 7 6 5 4 3 2 1

	Priority		
	low		high

49. Serves on the board of a social agency (such as Goodwill Industries, Salvation Army, Rescue Mission, YMCA).

10 9 8 7 6 5 4 3 2 1

50. Works personally for the election of good candidates for public office.

10 9 8 7 6 5 4 3 2 1

OTHER THINGS I EXPECT OF THE PASTOR:

OTHER THINGS I EXPECT OF THE CONGREGATION:

SCORE SHEETS

The questions in the Checklist are divided into ten categories of five questions each, dealing with different aspects of the life and work of church members and ministers. To compare scores among members or between members and the minister by various categories, simply write in the priority number you *circled* for Question 1 on the line beside Question 1 under the "Pastor" column on the next page.

Write the priority number you *underlined* on Question 1 under the "Lay" column for Question 1 below. All questions ending in "1" deal with the priestly aspects of the ministry. You may add each column to show how highly you rate priestly functions for your pastor and how highly you rate them for the laypersons of your church. Do the same for the other functional areas.

1 Priestly Ministry		2 Spiritual Life		3 Christian Education		4 Church Leadership		5 Group Process	
Pastor	Lay	Pastor	Lay	Pastor	Lay	Pastor	Lay	Pastor	Lay
1. ___	___	2. ___	___	3. ___	___	4. ___	___	5. ___	___
11. ___	___	12. ___	___	13. ___	___	14. ___	___	15. ___	___
21. ___	___	22. ___	___	23. ___	___	24. ___	___	25. ___	___
31. ___	___	32. ___	___	33. ___	___	34. ___	___	35. ___	___
41. ___	___	42. ___	___	43. ___	___	44. ___	___	45. ___	___
Totals		Totals		Totals		Totals		Totals	
___	___	___	___	___	___	___	___	___	___

6 Evangelism and Witnessing		7 Work Beyond Local Church		8 Service to Needy Persons		9 Work Through Social Agencies		10 Personal Agent of Social Change	
Pastor	Lay	Pastor	Lay	Pastor	Lay	Pastor	Lay	Pastor	Lay
6. ___	___	7. ___	___	8. ___	___	9. ___	___	10. ___	___
16. ___	___	17. ___	___	18. ___	___	19. ___	___	20. ___	___
26. ___	___	27. ___	___	28. ___	___	29. ___	___	30. ___	___
36. ___	___	37. ___	___	38. ___	___	39. ___	___	40. ___	___
46. ___	___	47. ___	___	48. ___	___	49. ___	___	50. ___	___
Totals		Totals		Totals		Totals		Totals	
___	___	___	___	___	___	___	___	___	___

WHAT NEXT?

Now go back to the questionnaire. Discover those questions which influenced the scores in special ways. In small groups, with the pastor present, try to develop an understanding and even a consensus as to what the pastor and the members reasonably ought to expect of themselves and of each other.

EXPLORING MEMBERSHIP ATTITUDES: A QUESTIONNAIRE SERVICE

A "Questionnaire for Local Church Planning" is an additional resource in Step 2:3 available as a service to users of this Manual. The contents of the questionnaire are shown on the succeeding pages. The service itself is described below and is available from: Office of Planning Resources, American Baptist National Ministries, Valley Forge, PA 19481.

1. If you wish to use the questionnaire as part of your planning, send to the above address an *up-to-date* resident membership list and indicate what percentage sample you wish used for the questionnaire. Normally 25 percent or 33 percent are the proportions of the membership used for a sample.

2. The Office of Planning Resources then uses a computer to create a random selection of your members. The questionnaire, accompanied by a return envelope and a postcard, is mailed directly to the persons in your membership sample.

3. Your church office is then sent a copy of the names being used in the sample. The postcard enclosed with the questionnaire is addressed to your church office and contains the message that the respondent has returned his/her questionnaire to the Valley Forge office.

4. You are asked to follow-up those members in the sample who have not returned their postcards to you within ten days. A phone follow-up is recommended.

5. When 50 percent to 70 percent of the questionnaires are returned to Valley Forge (usually 4 to 6 weeks), the Office of Planning Resources codes the results, runs them through a computer program, and prepares for you a report in two pieces: (1) a summary tabulation by three broad age groups (under-25, 25-to-49, 50-or-over), showing the actual percentage response to all items on the questionnaire; and (2) interpretive comments on the results.

This package service puts very helpful information into your hands.

The charge for the service is $125 plus 60¢ for each questionnaire used in the sample. You can quickly realize that most of this cost is spent for postage and printing. The remainder is the modest cost for computer tabulation. The service is being offered with no charge for staff time.

QUESTIONNAIRE FOR
LOCAL CHURCH PLANNING

You have been selected in a random sample of the members of your church to participate in this phase of the *planning process* in which your church is now engaged.

Most questions require only a √ in the appropriate box ☐ for your answer. Please be sure to answer all the questions since the validity of this survey depends on the completeness and the prompt return of your replies.

These questionnaires should be returned to Valley Forge for tabulation. No postage is required to return your form. Simply use the self-addressed, postage-free envelope provided.

PLEASE DO NOT SIGN YOUR NAME.

Your replies will be kept confidential, and the information you give will be used for statistical purposes only. At no time will individuals be identified with the answers. Only by achieving full returns from each one receiving this form can this phase of your planning effort be successful. Incidentally, the numbers next to each set of answers are to help the Valley Forge office count the answers. Please ignore them when checking your replies.

Thanks for your cooperation. Your answers to these questions are very important to us.

Prepared and distributed by
Office of Planning Resources
American Baptist National Ministries
Valley Forge, PA 19481

Let's begin with a few questions concerning your present church activities. Just put a check mark in the box □ next to your answer.

1. How long have you been a member of your present church?

Less than 1 year .... □¹	5 to 10 years .... □⁴
1 to 3 years .... □²	10 to 20 years .... □⁵
3 to 5 years .... □³	Over 20 years .... □⁶

2. Christians join churches for many reasons as they are led by God's spirit. How important was EACH OF THESE REASONS for you personally when you joined your present church?

	Very Important	Somewhat Important	Not Important
Enjoyed its friendly atmosphere	□¹	□²	□³
For the sake of my children	□¹	□²	□³
A place to serve others	□¹	□²	□³
Grew up in the church school	□¹	□²	□³
Program appealed to me	□¹	□²	□³
Invited to join by a member	□¹	□²	□³
Invited to join by the minister	□¹	□²	□³
Enjoyed the worship service	□¹	□²	□³
Liked the minister	□¹	□²	□³
Liked the people I met in church	□¹	□²	□³
Preferred the denomination	□¹	□²	□³
Followed example of a friend	□¹	□²	□³
Located conveniently near my home ..	□¹	□²	□³

3. In what denomination were you reared as a child? (Check only one).

American Baptist .... □⁰¹	Methodist .... □⁰⁷
Southern Baptist .... □⁰²	Presbyterian .... □⁰⁸
National Baptist .... □⁰³	Roman Catholic .... □⁰⁹
Disciples of Christ .... □⁰⁴	Other _____ □¹⁰
United Church of Christ .... □⁰⁵	None .... □¹¹
Lutheran .... □⁰⁶	

4. About what age were you when you first joined a church?

11 or under .... □¹	Older than 15, but under 21 □³
12 through 15 .... □²	21 or over .... □⁴

5. Generally speaking, how often each month do you attend the following in your church? (Check after each type of activity.)

	3 or more	Twice	Once	Less Often	Never	Not Offered
Major worship	□¹	□²	□³	□⁴	□⁵	□⁶
Other worship	□¹	□²	□³	□⁴	□⁵	□⁶
Mid-week service ...	□¹	□²	□³	□⁴	□⁵	□⁶
Church school	□¹	□²	□³	□⁴	□⁵	□⁶
Men-women-youth or mixed group meeting	□¹	□²	□³	□⁴	□⁵	□⁶
Board or committee	□¹	□²	□³	□⁴	□⁵	□⁶

6. Do you participate regularly in the following activities in YOUR church?

	Yes	No	Not Offered
Special study groups—not the church school	□¹	□²	□³
Special prayer groups—not the mid-week service	□¹	□²	□³
Family nights	□¹	□²	□³
Social action group	□¹	□²	□³
Retreats for church leaders	□¹	□²	□³
Special retreats for organized groups or total membership	□¹	□²	□³
Vacation church school	□¹	□²	□³
Visitation evangelism	□¹	□²	□³

7. Evaluate the effectiveness of current program in your church. (Check after each type of activity.)

	Good	Fair	Poor	Don't Know
Worship	□¹	□²	□³	□⁴
Christian education: children	□¹	□²	□³	□⁴
Christian education: youth	□¹	□²	□³	□⁴
Christian education: adults	□¹	□²	□³	□⁴
Fellowship	□¹	□²	□³	□⁴
Community ministry	□¹	□²	□³	□⁴
World mission support	□¹	□²	□³	□⁴

8. I wish my church had: (Check after each item.)

	Yes	No	Offered Now
New forms of worship	□¹	□²	□³
Mid-week service	□¹	□²	□³
Church school	□¹	□²	□³
A men's group	□¹	□²	□³
A social action group	□¹	□²	□³
Retreats for church leaders	□¹	□²	□³
Graded choirs	□¹	□²	□³
A women's group	□¹	□²	□³
A youth group for ____ ages	□¹	□²	□³
Study groups in homes	□¹	□²	□³

9. In what type of community did you grow up? (Check the one where you spent most of your childhood.)

On a farm .... □¹	City of 10,000 to 49,999 .. □⁴
Place of less than 2,500 . □²	City of 50,000 or more .... □⁵
Town of 2,500 to 9,999 .. □³	Suburb of a city of 50,000 or more .... □⁶

10. In what type of community do you live now?

On a farm .... □¹	City of 10,000 to 49,999 .. □⁴
Place of less than 2,500 . □²	City of 50,000 or more .... □⁵
Town of 2,500 to 9,999 .. □³	Suburb of a city of 50,000 or more .... □⁶

11. As a church member or participant, to what degree are you seeking help or guidance in the following areas of your life? (Check once after each.)

I want my church to help me . . .	Much	Some	Little
Be alert to needs of others in community	□¹	□²	□³
Give my children Christian education	□¹	□²	□³
Find meaning for personal existence	□¹	□²	□³
Know God's love and care for me	□¹	□²	□³
Meet my personal problems	□¹	□²	□³
Strengthen my faith and devotion	□¹	□²	□³
Express Christian vocation in my work	□¹	□²	□³
Work for justice in community and world	□¹	□²	□³
Understand the Bible	□¹	□²	□³
Understand Christian doctrine	□¹	□²	□³
Use my leisure time more effectively	□¹	□²	□³
Become trained as an effective lay leader	□¹	□²	□³

12. Indicate which of the following local church responsibilities you have or have had in the last five years:

	Have responsibility now	Had responsibility in past
Church officer	□¹	□²
Board member	□¹	□²
Committee member	□¹	□²
Church school teacher	□¹	□²
Small group leader	□¹	□²
Home visitation	□¹	□²
Choir	□¹	□²
Usher	□¹	□²
Officer of church organization	□¹	□²
Other _____	□¹	□²

13. Which of the following should be responsibilities for your church? (Check once after each item.)

	Yes	No	Not Sure
Teaching the Bible	□¹	□²	□³
Working for racial or ethnic justice and equality	□¹	□²	□³
Helping young people	□¹	□²	□³
Encouraging personal involvement in community organization	□¹	□²	□³
Helping people make their occupation Christian	□¹	□²	□³
Effecting change in government policies	□¹	□²	□³
Caring for needs of older people	□¹	□²	□³
Fostering devotional life	□¹	□²	□³
Supporting home and foreign missions	□¹	□²	□³

14. Housing you live in. (Check only one.)

Single family dwelling □¹	Nursing or retirement home □⁴
Apartment □²	Dormitory □⁵
Mobile home □³	Other _____ □⁶

15. In your personal life, do you engage in devotional practice?

Regularly □¹   Sometimes □².   Never □³

In the next set of questions we're turning to some questions dealing with your understanding of the church and its ministry. We want you to express your attitude or opinion. Simply check the best answers that come to your mind.

16. How necessary do you feel it is for a Christian to believe or do the following? (Check once after each item.)

	Necessary	Desirable	Not Necessary
Accept church creeds	□¹	□²	□³
Be an active church member	□¹	□²	□³
Attend Sunday worship regularly	□¹	□²	□³
Believe in Jesus as Savior	□¹	□²	□³
Have a specific conversion experience	□¹	□²	□³
Be baptized	□¹	□²	□³
Obey the Ten Commandments	□¹	□²	□³
Pray and read the Bible daily	□¹	□²	□³
Work for social justice	□¹	□²	□³
Contribute to the church	□¹	□²	□³
Follow Christ as Lord in daily life	□¹	□²	□³
Speak in tongues	□¹	□²	□³

17. I believe my church and my denomination should cooperate with other churches and other denominations: (Check once after each item.)

	Yes	No	Not sure
At the local level	□¹	□²	□³
At the regional and state level	□¹	□²	□³
At the national level	□¹	□²	□³

18. Check below what you consider to be appropriate ways for the church to react to community problems:

Not be involved directly	□¹
Move no faster than the neighborhood in which it is located	□¹
Deal with the question **only** in sermons or study groups	□¹
Individuals may work on special projects at their own initiative	□¹
Changing attitudes of individuals in the church	□¹
Form special **action** groups to work on crisis problems	□¹
Lead the community to solve its problems	□¹

19. Check your opinion as to the category that best describes each statement given below: (Check once after each item.)

	True	Probably True	Probably Not True	Not True
All persons are born with a sinful nature	□¹	□²	□³	□⁴
All persons are equal in the sight of God	□¹	□²	□³	□⁴
God answers prayer	□¹	□²	□³	□⁴
God revealed himself to humanity in Jesus Christ	□¹	□²	□³	□⁴
Hell is a just punishment for sinners	□¹	□²	□³	□⁴
Jesus rose from the dead	□¹	□²	□³	□⁴
Jesus was born of a virgin	□¹	□²	□³	□⁴
Sin is separation from God	□¹	□²	□³	□⁴
The Bible is the Word of God	□¹	□²	□³	□⁴
The Church is the Body of Christ	□¹	□²	□³	□⁴
There is life after death	□¹	□²	□³	□⁴
We are justified by faith	□¹	□²	□³	□⁴

20. How long have you been a member of your present denomination? .

Less than 1 year □¹   3 to 5 years ..... □³   10 to 20 years .. □⁵
1 to 3 years ..... □²   5 to 10 years ... □⁴   More than 20 years .... □⁶

21. How helpful has your church actually been to you in the following areas of your life? (Check once after each item.)

In helping me to:	Much	Some	Little
Be alert to needs of others in community	□¹	□²	□³
Give my children Christian education	□¹	□²	□³
Find meaning for personal existence	□¹	□²	□³
Know God's love and care for me	□¹	□²	□³
Meet my personal problems	□¹	□²	□³
Strengthen my faith and devotion	□¹	□²	□³
Express Christian vocation in my work	□¹	□²	□³
Work for justice in community and world	□¹	□²	□³
Understand the Bible	□¹	□²	□³
Understand Christian doctrine	□¹	□²	□³
Use my leisure time more effectively	□¹	□²	□³
Become trained as an effective lay leader	□¹	□²	□³

22. Local churches should undertake the following cooperative involvements:

	Yes	No	Not Sure
Joint services of worship	□¹	□²	□³
Pastoral exchanges	□¹	□²	□³
Interchurch parishes	□¹	□²	□³
Joint programs of education	□¹	□²	□³
Participate in councils of churches	□¹	□²	□³
Participate in community betterment efforts	□¹	□²	□³

23. What is your personal attitude toward each of the following statements?

	Agree	Disagree	Not Sure
Your church should be willing to receive anyone as members regardless of race or culture	□¹	□²	□³
Your minister should have a right to preach on controversial subjects	□¹	□²	□³
There should be complete separation of church and state	□¹	□²	□³
Prayers should be allowed in public schools	□¹	□²	□³
Public schools should offer classes in the world's religions	□¹	□²	□³
Churches should support minorities in their struggle to achieve civil rights	□¹	□²	□³
Christians should refrain from using alcoholic beverages	□¹	□²	□³
Denominations have a right to issue policy statements on social matters	□¹	□²	□³

24. How should major decisions be made in the local church?. (Check only one.)

By majority rule upon formal vote .... □¹
By church leaders .... □²
By the pastor .... □³
By discussion until consensus is achieved .... □⁴

25. Check the statement that **best** describes what you consider to be the chief responsibility of a pastor. (Check only one.)

Minister to the needs of the members .... ☐1
Help prepare members to serve within the church organization .... ☐2
Help prepare members to serve in the community .... ☐3
Provide leadership through worship and preaching .... ☐4
Seek to enlarge the membership .... ☐5
Represent the congregation in the community .... ☐6
Promote denominational programs .... ☐7

26. Check the statement that **best** describes the chief responsibility of the lay member of the church. (Check only one.)

Attend services regularly and support the church financially .... ☐1
Accept designated leadership roles in the church so the minister can give time to other work .... ☐2
Use his/her talents to serve in the community in the name of Christ as an individual citizen .... ☐3
Participate in church-sponsored actions to bring about community change .... ☐4

27. Below is a list of functions that are among those currently being carried out by local churches. What is your reaction to each one?

	Do affirm and would (do) participate	Do affirm but would not personally participate	Could not affirm
Visitation evangelism	☐1	☐2	☐3
Contacting church shut-ins	☐1	☐2	☐3
Fellowship activities of church groups	☐1	☐2	☐3
Sponsor a youth fellowship	☐1	☐2	☐3
Contribute to a civil rights organization	☐1	☐2	☐3
Counseling on abortion and its alternatives	☐1	☐2	☐3
Sponsor a group-care facility for parolees	☐1	☐2	☐3
Support boycotts for farm or industrial products where workers are exploited	☐1	☐2	☐3
Lobby for the right to die of individuals who are incurably ill	☐1	☐2	☐3
Design a takeover of a corrupt local political structure	☐1	☐2	☐3

28. In the area of public affairs, which of the following are the most critical issues today? (Select the THREE most important and enter the letters in the boxes.)

a. Quality Public Education
b. Highway Safety
c. Control Inflation
d. Respect for Authority
e. Adequate Jobs
f. Criminal Justice and Penal Reform
g. Achieving World Peace
h. Quality Housing
i. Environmental Quality
j. Welfare Reform
k. Quality Health Care
l. Police Protection for my Family
m. A Trustworthy Government
n. Achieving Racial Justice
o. Solution to the Drug and Alcohol Problem
p. Pride in America
q. Other _____

Your 1st choice _____   Your 2nd choice _____   Your 3rd choice _____

29. How do you rate your loyalty to the denomination of which you are now a member? (Check only one.)

Very strong .... ☐1   Denomination does
Strong .... ☐2   not matter to me .... ☐4
Weak .... ☐3

Now we'd like to ask you a few personal questions about yourself. Most of these answers can be checked very quickly.

30. What is your age? (Please check one.)

Under 18 .... ☐1   25 to 39 .... ☐3   50 to 64 .... ☐5
18 to 24 .... ☐2   40 to 49 .... ☐4   65 or over .... ☐6

31. What is your sex? (Please check one.)

Male ..... ☐1   Female ..... ☐2

32. With whom do you live? (Check only one.)

Alone . . . . ☐1
With spouse only . . . . ☐2
With spouse and children . . . . ☐3
As child with parents . . . . ☐4
Other _____ ☐5

33. What is your race? (Please check one.)

Black .... ☐1   White .... ☐3
Oriental .... ☐2   Other _____ ☐4

34. Education (Check your highest attainment.)

I am still in school .... ☐¹	Completed Trade or Skill	
Less than 5 years ....☐²	School .... ☐⁶	
5 to 8 years .... ☐³	Some College .... ☐⁷	
9 to 12 years .... ☐⁴	Completed College .... ☐⁸	
Completed High School .... ☐⁵	Post-graduate Education	
	(Degree _____).......... ☐⁹	

35. At the present time do you participate in any of the following types of non-church organizations?

	Yes	No
Art, drama, literary	☐¹	☐²
Business or management organization	☐¹	☐²
Charitable or social service group	☐¹	☐²
Civil rights group (NAACP, SCLC, etc.)	☐¹	☐²
Community or neighborhood organization	☐¹	☐²
Fraternal organization (lodges, etc.)	☐¹	☐²
Farmers' or labor union	☐¹	☐²
Political party organization	☐¹	☐²
Professional organization	☐¹	☐²
School or education group (PTA, AAUW, etc.)	☐¹	☐²
Service or civic group (Rotary, Kiwanis, etc.)	☐¹	☐²
Social or recreational group	☐¹	☐²

36. What is the total number of organizations **outside your local church** to which you belong?

None .... ☐¹	Three .... ☐⁴
One .... ☐²	Four .... ☐⁵
Two .... ☐³	Five or more .... ☐⁶

37. Of your five closest friends, how many are also members of your local church?

None .... ☐¹	Three .... ☐⁴
One .... ☐²	Four .... ☐⁵
Two .... ☐³	Five .... ☐⁶

38. Present status (Check only one.)

Homemaker .... ☐¹	Employed .... ☐³	Unemployed .... ☐⁵
Student .... ☐²	Retired .... ☐⁴	

39. If now employed, what is your type of work? The classifications used below are those of the U.S. Bureau of the Census. If you are uncertain, describe the occupation as fully as you can in the margin.

Clerical and related workers: bookkeepers, stenographers, cashiers, mail carriers, shipping clerks, secretaries, ticket agents, telephone operators, office machine operators, etc. .... ☐⁰¹

Craftsmen, foremen, and related workers: tinsmiths, bakers, carpenters, masons, shoemakers, electricians, inspectors, cement workers, jewelers, machinist, etc. .... ☐⁰²

Farmers and farm managers .... ☐⁰³

Farm laborers and farm foremen .... ☐⁰⁴

Laborers: garage laborers, car washers, stevedores, lumbermen, teamsters, gardeners, unskilled helpers in construction, manufacturing, fishing, etc. .... ☐⁰⁵

Operatives and related workers: chauffeurs, delivery men, laundry workers, apprentices, meat cutters, semi-skilled and unskilled workers in manufacturing establishments, etc. .... ☐⁰⁶

Private household workers: servants, laundresses, employed housekeepers, etc. .... ☐⁰⁷

Professional, technical and related workers: teachers, editors, dentists, clergymen, professors, doctors, architects, librarians, accountants, photographers, dancers, surveyors, chiropractors, athletes, etc. .... ☐⁰⁸

Proprietors, managers and officials: public officials, credit men, buyers, officers, floor managers, proprietors, railroad conductors, etc. .... ☐⁰⁹

Sales workers: salesmen, insurance and real estate agents and brokers, stock and bond salesmen, demonstrators, news-boys, etc. .... ☐¹⁰

Services workers: policemen, barbers, janitors, beauticians, porters, waiters, ushers, etc. .... ☐¹¹

Other (write in) _____ .... ☐¹²

40. What was your TOTAL FAMILY income last year?

Under $3,000 .... ☐¹	$10,000 to 14,999 .... ☐⁴
$3,000 to 4,999 .... ☐²	$15,000 to 19,999 .... ☐⁵
$5,000 to 9,999 .... ☐³	$20,000 to 29,999 .... ☐⁶
	$30,000 or more .... ☐⁷

41. How many contributed to the total income reported above?

One ...☐¹	Two ....☐²	Three or more ....☐³

247

42. Please add anything you would like to say.

_____

_____

_____

_____

_____

_____

_____

_____

_____

_____

_____

_____

_____

_____

_____

_____

_____

_____

This is the end of the questionnaire. Thanks for your cooperation. After checking your answers, please use the postage-free envelope to return your questionnaire to Valley Forge.

Local Church Planning Manual

32087

William Jessup University
Library
333 Sunset Blvd.
Rocklin, CA 95765

32087